C0-AYF-417

College Athletic Scholarships

College Athletic Scholarships

A Complete Guide

by
Bob Mauro

McFarland & Company, Inc., Publishers
Jefferson, North Carolina, and London

GV
583
M33
1988

Library of Congress Cataloguing-in-Publication Data are available

Library of Congress Catalog Number Card 87-43210

ISBN 0-89950-328-4 (acid-free natural paper)

© 1988 Bob Mauro. All rights reserved.

Manufactured in the United States of America.

McFarland & Company, Inc., Publishers
  Box 611, Jefferson, North Carolina 28640

3 3001 00719 1132

To Sharon
Thanks for all your help and support

Contents

Preface

Each year deserving male and female high school athletes from all parts of the United States are not recruited by any college or university. Aside from a lack of true athletic talent, the foremost reason for the young athlete's unsuccessful quest to win scholarship money is the lack of knowledge to follow a methodical step-by-step approach to market the athlete's special abilities. Total awareness, another key need, is built into the structure of this book so the reader will better be able to analyze all aspects of the step-by-step process. If the athlete has the talent, but does not have the awareness to improve that talent or the approach to sell his or her skills, the athlete will often fall short in winning the reward of scholarship assistance. The purpose of this book is to provide a complete and practical resource for information which can lead a concerned high school coach or deserving young athlete to use all available resources to his or her useful advantage to win an athletic scholarship. It will also prove to be helpful for the athlete who is successful in being offered a grant-in-aid.

Since my entire life has centered around playing and coaching sports, I have a keen interest in young people with accelerated abilities and athletic backgrounds. An athletic scholarship gave me an opportunity to go to college and, in turn, the opportunity to pursue professional pursuits which I enjoy. Had it not been for an athletic scholarship I might be "digging ditches" in my home state of New Jersey today.

Each year talented athletes benefit from college scholarships. Much has been said about scholarships; nothing to my knowledge has been written to aid deserving young men and young women to have a greater understanding of the total recruiting process of all aspects of college athletic scholarships. The emphasis of this text is not only on the "how" to gain attention to your skills. It will candidly discuss "why" scholarships are awarded. "What" to look for is also a key topic of discussion. "How" to go after your goal of gaining this prestigious reward is the thrust behind the writing of this publication.

The athlete must also be very aware of the many important factors involved in selecting the proper school for himself or herself. Being a college athlete is much more demanding than being simply a college student. The athlete who is unhappy after matriculation to a college probably did not fully investigate the program he/she entered. Every attempt has been made to completely analyze each of the important factors an athlete must use in selecting a college.

This book is not only a reference but a guide. Topics covered include the following:

- Knowledge of the types of scholarships offered
- An athlete's approach to bettering his/her skills
- Experiences of former athletes in selecting college athletic programs
- Answers to the most commonly asked questions in recruiting
- Signing of a scholarship
- How to find the most up-to-date rules of recruiting

- Problems created when an athlete signs more than one scholarship
- How to locate college athletic programs who field teams in your sport
- How the coach, the player and an interested third party can properly help in the recruiting of the deserving athlete
- How the athlete can systematically select the best sports program for himself/herself
- Knowing why you shouldn't quit in your pursuit of an athletic scholarship

After reading this text you will be much more aware of the entire athletic environment. Extensive technical language has been deliberately avoided. Terms have been defined when necessary. Every attempt has been made to be direct, concise and easily understandable so the reader can utilize the contents with a maximum degree of efficiency.

For the sake of making the book easier reading, I have attempted to direct many of the remarks directly to the athlete, or the coach when appropriate. Many references have been to males, but you young women—the opportunity is just as great for you!

Chapter I
The Athlete

Many years ago the athlete played any team oriented sport for the love of that sport and for the glory he could bring to his school. The athlete gained limited recognition if he was exceptional. In the early 1900s only a handful of universities participated in a limited number of sports. Most collegiate sports teams were actually "club" teams or pickup teams coached by one of the team members. Football seasons often consisted of one, two or three games. Women in sports were virtually nonexistent. How things have changed!

Today, athletes still play for love, glory and recognition; however, the athletic teams and athletes themselves are much better coached and understand more about their sports. High schools now offer a choice of many sports to all students as a part of their interscholastic athletic programs. Collegiate programs travel extensively and spend great amounts of money to recruit the most talented high school performers. Professional teams recruit the collegiate stars.

The easiest way to explain the difference in yesterday's teams and today's teams is with one word: MONEY. Due to increased interest and enlarged gate receipts, each level of sports participation (youth, junior high, high school, college, and professional) has benefited from a tremendous infusion of money to improve the quality of what is now a very big U.S. industry—sports at all levels. This book discusses the high school-to-college transition. This chapter discusses the athlete and the demands he experiences, the high school athlete's role as he prepares for his collegiate future, and how each athlete readies himself for his collegiate experience. As the athlete is discussed, the reader should understand that this reading should serve as a guide to what lies ahead for a talented individual.

Reading this chapter of this book will not ensure any athlete a scholarship or grant-in-aid to a college or university. Rather, it should heighten each reader's overall awareness as to what can be expected of an athlete as well as what an athlete can expect. Remember, any athlete who is fortunate enough to be considered for a grant-in-aid must be a very talented performer.

If you have exceptional natural talent and the desire to improve that talent, you possess the two most basic attributes necessary to be a viable candidate to play a collegiate sport. Of course the specific skills that you possess need to be on a par with, or be better than, those skills of the athletes in the college(s) you are considering. The justification for this "par or better" philosophy is basic. Let us look at the sport of swimming for example. Swimmers continue to improve each year on the best times and marks set by their predecessors. In 1978 the National Collegiate Athletic Association Championship Tournament saw male swimmers from all parts of the United States break two national records out of 17 events. This is an increasingly common accomplishment. A more thorough 1978 analysis established that the oldest record in the National Collegiate Athletic Association's (NCAA–men) record book was only two years old! During the same year in the Association of Intercollegiate Athletics for

Women (NCAA–women) Swimming Championships, 17 of 19 records fell! Similar studies show that the oldest record in the Association of Intercollegiate Athletics for Women's record book was only three years old. (The AIAW is now defunct, and is currently called the NCAA Women's Division.) Citing these facts demonstrates examples of the improvement which is occurring in collegiate swimming circles. Swimming marks are measurements of time which are easily observable.

Study measurable statistics in other sports and you will notice very similar improvements. National records show that field goal accuracy in basketball improves annually. More and more collegiate athletes are making it to the major leagues in baseball. Each sport's athletes show measurable evidence of improvement.

Today's athlete continues to improve. The athlete is stronger and faster due to improved methods of training and conditioning; he is coached better in the specific skills and techniques of the game he plays. Due to the tremendous availability of teaching aids like books and films, today's athlete is more knowledgeable about his sport specialty. These teaching aids help both the athlete and his coach. Today's athlete is putting more time into his sport—often specializing in one sport as early as the sophomore year in high school.

The readers of this book will generally be prospective scholarship-type high school student-athletes. Some will be seniors and some will be freshmen. To be successful each reader must only concern himself with his own academic and athletic progress—one year at a time. No matter what your age now, you must prepare yourself for your graduation from high school. Look objectively at your talents and abilities so you might clearly evaluate the skills which you need to improve.

In order to improve, the athlete must use constructive criticism to his advantage for both athletic and academic success. Remember, only the strong survive in the highly competitive world of athletics.

As discussed at the outset of this chapter, you need two basic qualities to play on the collegiate level. The first is God-given talent. Since your body type, height and athletic ability were determined before you were born, there is no way to change these essential ingredients. The second quality is to have the desire to improve on your natural abilities. This desire for improvement is the quality that you yourself control. No one else knows you better than you know yourself. You know your talents, your strengths and your weaknesses. If you have the talent to excel in a sport, you are aware of it soon after you begin to play that sport. The key to success then rests on your shoulders. You must master the skills necessary to become an outstanding participant in the sport or sports that you choose to play. The attempt to master the sport continues each year, making each year of performance equally important in the athlete's progress.

Freshman and sophomore athletes should be hard working, dedicated student-athletes, with the latter trying to improve on freshman performance marks in the playing field and in the classroom. The sophomore should challenge himself to turn freshman weaknesses into sophomore strengths. Junior athletes should be even more dedicated—working to improve work habits in both practice and game situations, as well as to continue mastering the academic half of their student-athlete life. Seniors must be at their best. Seniors are always being tested for both individual achievements as well as leadership potential. But don't forget, seniors, graduation from high school and retirement are not one and the same for a scholarship athlete. Seniors should strive for the same levels of improvement over junior year performance as junior athletes expect of themselves over the sophomore year. No one said being an athlete was easy, did they?

Many college recruiters around the country believe that the junior year of high school is the most important year for an athlete to be successful. By having an outstanding junior year, you have the opportunity to make the college recruiter's *recruiting list*. This recruiting list is a listing of the best game-tested talent in the school's specific recruiting area. This list is usually made after the coaching staff has had the opportunity to observe game performances or after having received extremely high coaching recommendations about specific, talented athletes based on their junior year performances. If you play well in more than one sport, you may be on the list in two sports at the same college. This doubles your chances to meet your goal of achieving a scholarship.

Making a collegiate recruiting list or earning recommendations to many programs is important because it affords the athlete
the chance to be evaluated by as many schools as possible. But
making this list is not the payoff! As a junior you still have a long
way to go before you graduate. In many cases the junior athlete
will not even know he is on such a recruiting list. Many times colleges will choose not to contact you until after your senior year
begins. And, as I have said, being on a recruiting list carries no
financial award.

The most important item to keep in mind about your junior
year is your continued improvement. That's right. Improvement
should be the foremost word in your goal-oriented vocabulary.

When observing behavioral characteristics of people in our
society we find that no one seems to act exactly the same as new
demands are made of each person. An athlete's performance "will
either get better or will get worse" to quote Notre Dame's Lou
Holtz, who was one of my college coaches and later my boss.
Constantly, we see that the demands of new competition keep the
athlete constantly changing. Sports performances are always in
the state of dynamic change. New stars develop, picking up the
slack when more experienced people falter. The star junior
athlete who has attained recruiting-list status must improve his
skills continually or he will find himself slipping into a barely
passable performance and being passed by players with lesser
abilities who make the improvement mentioned from the junior
season to the senior season.

Let me suggest some ideas which I believe will help you during your junior year to show constant improvement: (1) Prepare
yourself well for your junior season and play to your fullest
capability. Never waste an opportunity in practices or games to
work toward improvement. (2) Be constantly aware of coaching
points and details given by your coach because your knowledge
plus fundamental skills will create speed and efficiency in your
performance. (3) Be a smart listener and a good doer. Listening
helps you to learn the strategies and increase your knowledge of
the game. Doing goes hand-in-hand with listening. Combining
what you have learned with your physical talents leads to a good
performance. (4) Immediately following your junior season, talk

to your coach about your goals. Be open and frank. Ask him to be straightforward when he evaluates your progress. Ask your coach if he thinks you have the potential to play in college, should you successfully improve your skills. Develop a plan of attack to improve necessary areas like conditioning, strength or speed. Carry out your plan of attack. The athlete must arduously prepare himself for a great senior season.

During your senior year, you have the opportunity to show the finished product of your athletic skills. You must demonstrate your specialty with excellence and determination. Many athletes are recommended as scholarship candidiates before each year begins, but the athletes who perform the best during the senior season are the winners in the battle for the financial grants that are awarded.

You must be made aware of a pitfall common to senior athletes from all parts of the country. The senior athlete is in an unfortunate situation since he can only compete against the teams in his league or conference in his geographical location. When any athlete excels against the competition in his league or conference opponents, his credentials and achievements may be excellent. Team, local, county, and state honors may be plentiful to reward your outstanding achievements. But when you are being considered for a college scholarship, your talents are being compared with the talents of players or performers from many geographical locations. Simply because you are the best player in your area, you may not be the best in your position or your specialty from a larger geographical area. Never be completely satisfied with your performance. Don't just coast to win. Be a dominating performer against every opponent each time you compete. If you do your best and perform consistently, you will be taking a great step in achieving the goal of winning a college athletic scholarship.

Chapter II
Evaluation

The opportunity to win a collegiate athletic scholarship is very much a responsibility as well as a privlege. When you are considered for a scholarship many factors are considered, as you might well have gleaned from the first chapter. But let's look at you in a realistic and exacting way—let's evaluate your athletic potentials honestly and realistically.

An athletic scholarship is a reward for a job well done. In order to come under consideration you must have some God-given talents. The real key to your success rests not so much in your potential, but in what you have already accomplished and what you continue to accomplish throughout your high school career. You must have lofty goals and systematically improve the skills that allow you to achieve the goals you have set. Winning a scholarship is a very lofty goal, but certainly attainable.

Now let's take a closer look at you. It was said by Paul Dietzel, who coached LSU to a national football championship, "There are two people you can't fool: you can't fool yourself, and you can't fool the Lord." How right he was with this statement. The abilities and deficiencies you were born with are yours and yours alone. The biggest challenge you face right now is to recognize each. It would take chapters and chapters to detail a plan for each person reading this publication to improve his athletic deficiencies and enhance the abilities he has already. I would like to leave that information to the professional personnel of each specific sport. With a trip to a bookstore or library, I trust you can find publications which deal with expert instruction in various skills peculiar to your sports speciality. If not, I would suggest you discuss your desire to learn more about specific sport skills with your coach for his or her recommendations for reading materials. Books concerned with coaching are excellent; each deals with specific skills and how to improve each skill as well as philosophical and conceptual aspects of the particular sport in question.

An interested athlete who aspires to win a scholarship should work to become an expert in his specialty, just as a student who aspires to win an academic scholarship in engineering works to excel in high-level mathematics courses. They only difference in the athlete-engineer comparison is that the engineer probably won't require any physical skills to win his scholarship. The athlete's requirements span athletic skill levels and knowledge, as well as academic proficiency.

Let's expand an example of a method of self-evaluation which encompasses many of the athletic attributes required. Use this example and create (with your coach) your own self-evaluation form. It can be a helpful tool to better understand your needs as well as your abilities. You need an unbiased partner to work with you to "grade" your self-test results, since everyone has a slightly different viewpoint of what is excellent. We all tend to think we are doing the right things; therefore, an unbiased test partner can help with a second opinion for constructive criticism. Athletes who do not like constructive criticism of their abilities are usually athletes who don't improve the skills and attitudes necessary to go to the next level of competition, in this case the collegiate level.

Johnny Doaks' Self-Evaluation—Junior Year

Trait	Outstanding	Excellent	Good	Fair	Poor
Desire to win	1	2	3	4	5
Self-motivation	1	2	3	4	5
Team scheme play	1	2	3	4	5
Helping others	1	2	3	4	5
Cooperation with staff	1	2	3	4	5
Attitude in practice	1	2	3	4	5
Attitude in games	1	2	3	4	5
Toughness	1	2	3	4	5
Strength	1	2	3	4	5
Height and Weight	1	2	3	4	5
Speed	1	2	3	4	5
Mental mistakes	1	2	3	4	5

Let's take a closer look at hypothetical athlete Johnny Doaks in the example above. Johnny is a rising senior football player at Smithfield High School. He plays linebacker and is 6'1" tall, weighs 205 pounds and runs a 5.0 forty-yard dash. He has a great nose for the football; therefore, he is in on a great number of tackles for his team. Just making tackles or getting good press recognition will not get him to college. But the manner in which he plays linebacker will. Linebackers are supposed to make tackles. So let's evaluate some of the things Johnny might do to improve his play and self-evaluation of his talents.

It has been said by many football coaches that "you don't measure a football player by height and weight or inches and pounds." There usually is a tremendous open-mindedness in the minds of coaches who evaluate films on what it takes to make a great linebacker. Let's go into Johnny's thought process of self-evaluation by making a checklist of abilities ("1" being the highest and "5" being the lowest). It is quite obvious that no one is a complete "1," or, on the same thought process, no one is a complete

"5." But it is also very obvious that only truthful self-evaluation can aid your chances to utilize the results to improve areas of weakness. By using Johnny's self-evaluation as an example, let's see what all this means. I think the above example will help clarify some of the thought process which is done on each athlete who is offered a scholarship.

1. *Desire to win.* No one likes to lose and Johnny thinks he is not an exception. He rated himself a "1" because ever since he was a youth he competed to win and wanted to win. He has always played for championship-calibre teams throughout his career and feels that his contribution was a key factor for his teams' successes.

A true "1" evaluation in this category is an athlete who demonstrates the ability to be both a great practice player as well as an exceptional game player. He is one who is constantly trying to improve his techniques, to learn his assignments diligently, and rarely has to be told twice to do anything. He is always to practice on time and volunteers to do anything "extra" to make his team win.

2. *Self-motivation.* Johnny attends all practice sessions but needs to be prodded to finish his sprints or to learn his assignments for the next session. He needs to be reminded that he must continue his preseason workout plan or to learn important down-and-distance tendencies provided in the coaching staff's weekly game plan.

A "1" in self-motivation never needs reminders. He leads; he does not follow. He treats his football learning assignments with the devotion he applies to making an "A" in algebra. He exceeds the coaching staff's team expectations in the weight room, in off-season conditioning, in preseason practices, as well as in game situations. He never needs prodding, and he asks for extra help.

3. *Desire to play in the team scheme.* Johnny rated himself a "3." He is generally good, but he knows that he frequently likes to overplay his position to assist another teammate and it sometimes costs the team expensive yardage. He also tends to second-guess his coaching staff on occasion, and it tends to confuse his "real" assignment from his "supposed" assignment.

A "1" rating in this category is reserved for the football player who is an excellent assignment player. He is the linebacker that is responsible to fill his hole, the guard who traps the proper person, or the back who runs to the proper area—and then makes his cut. A "1" player willingly plays a second playing position or alternate playing position if it is in the team's best interest. The top team players also applaud other team members' accomplishments.

4. *Willingness to help others.* Johnny rated himself a "1" because he thought that his ability to do his assignment and the player's next to him, too, was good. I think he very much overevaluated himself here and measured himself with the wrong viewpoint. Willingness to help others means assisting those around him to succeed. A championship team very rarely is a one-man show. Championships are won by teammates playing together. And recruiters are looking for players who will fit into their team concept.

A true "1" is the athlete who learns his assignment and the assignments of those around him so that when a situation occurs in a game that creates confusion in a younger player's mind, the older one will know his assignment and help. He shares his knowledge of the opponent or of his position with others.

5. *Cooperation with coaching staff.* Johnny rated himself a "3" because he sometimes does and sometimes doesn't cooperate. He likes to challenge the system because he wants to be the center of attention.

If Johnny is to attain the status of being a "number 1" in this category, he must not only follow the staff's direction, but lead his younger mates through his actions. Remember we discussed that he needed prodding? "1's" do whatever it takes or do whatever the staff wants and support those requirements when interfacing with their teammates and staff members.

6. *Attitude in practice.* Johnny rated himself an honest "3" because he doesn't think that all practices are important. He "saves" himself for the game.

A "1" rating here may be the most important of all. Whether you believe it or not, your play in the game directly correlates to your efforts in practice. Recruiters would rather know how you play in practice than any other aspect of your evaluation, because at higher levels of competition it is your practice habits that make you an excellent performer. Great teams and great players are great practicers, too.

7. *Attitude in game situation.* Almost every athlete will rate himself a "1" here. Johnny is no exception. He chose a top rating because he totally exhausts himself in games and plays with fury. Most athletes do.

Let me remind you that you may think you're a "1" here, but if you don't do all the extras in practice, I seriously doubt if you will be a "1" to the observer who is looking at your play on film. For the record, an athlete who "stands around" a lot, never showing extra effort or good technique, will get poor marks from the observer.

8. *Toughness.* Johnny loves to hit people. He gave himself a "1" on that characteristic alone. But there are two types of toughness—physical and mental.

Physically tough athletes like to challenge the opponent by running through blocks, breaking tackles or dragging the opponent into the end zone for a TD. Mentally tough players play well when they are tired or hurt (minor injury). I think the best evaluations I ever received regarding athletes in football were those discussing what a player does on the last series of downs in the fourth quarter of a close game. You may think the recruiter stays the whole game to shake your coach's hand at the end of the game or let it be known that he was there to watch you. His evaluation process places strong emphasis on mental toughness. A player with great mental toughness is always a great practicer.

9. *Strength.* Johnny is not superstrong but feels he is above average. He works fairly hard in the weight room, and bench presses the third highest amount on the team. He dominates all the smaller opponents and fares well with the big ones. His self-evaluation of "2"is probably fair.

A "1" in strength is somewhat measurable by weight room statistics, but is better evaluated by performance. The runner who breaks tackles constantly is strong. The linebacker who knocks runners backward is strong. The offensive lineman who always goes forward on a drive block is strong. Basketball's strong rebounders, volleyball's strong spikers, soccer's strong kickers, and baseball's strong pitching arms are different examples of strength.

10. *Height and weight.* Height is inherited and weight is 90 percent inherited. Johnny's self-measurement of "2" is fair.

If you want to know what a true "1" rating is, simply find a *professional* football squad and observe the heights at each position. Most athletes who are high school seniors will not grow any taller. Weight can improve with proper diet and certainly through the maturation years of 18–21. I think a good rule of thumb is that if you are within 10 percent of the weight of the collegiate athlete who plays the same position, you are probably a "1." Since height is a big concern of all recruited athletes (especially in football), let's discuss typical heights of major college players. A back is usually 5′10½″–6′1″, although the best back I was ever associated with—Ted Brown—was a first round draft choice of the Minnesota Vikings at 5′9″. Down lineman range from 6′1″ to 6′6″. Linebacker types range from 6′0″–6′4″. Wide receivers and tight ends are usually 5′11″–6′3″ and 6′2″–6′4″, respectively. A defensive back is usually from 5′9″ to 6′1″. Kickers are any size, but punters are preferred in the 6′0″–6′2″ range.

11. *Speed.* Johnny rated himself too high. He rated himself a "1" because he was the fastest linebacker on his team, but, compared to the major college standards, he was average at best.

Using the same position-by-position breakdown listed earlier, and measured in the 40-yard dash on grass, here are some guidelines on achieving a "1" rating:

- Offensive backs—4.4–4.7 seconds
- Defensive backs—4.4–4.8 seconds
- Down lineman (offensive)—4.9–5.2 seconds
- Down lineman (defensive)—4.7–5.0 seconds
- Linebackers—4.7–4.9 seconds
- Receivers—4.4–4.6 seconds and tight ends—4.7–4.9 seconds
- Kickers and punters—5.1 seconds and under

12. *Mental Mistakes.* Johnny rated himself a "2" because he seldom missed assignments and seldom let down-and-distance situations hamper his play.

A perfect rating goes to the athlete who *rarely* misses assignments and *always* knows the down-and-distance tendencies of his opponent. Again, the key measuring point is how well he performs mentally in the fourth quarter when he is very tired. A proven athlete does his assignments when the game is on the line. Jumping offsides in football or committing a walking violation in basketball are examples of mental mistakes.

No matter what team sport you desire to evaluate, the same attitudes should be applicable to this example. Only height, weight, and speed requirements may vary. The self-evaluation is the best method to evaluate your skills and attitudes, but do get a second opinion from an unbiased person. (Your coach is your best choice.) The unbiased decision affords the athlete a correction factor which will make the evaluation more useful.

What do you do with the results? Work on the weaknesses. There is always time to improve.

Let's do another type of evaluation. This type of evaluation is a more technical one regarding the actual skills performed in a contest. Its evaluator can respond to the questions with either objective or subjective answers, but with either we can create a corrective action recommendation for skill improvement.

This different style of evaluation was done by hypothetical baseball player Patrick Cobb. Note that Patrick evaluates a skill with an objective, measurable statistic, a subjective comment, and a corrective action measurement. Notice also that specific goals are made for the next season. Remember that Patrick is a hypothetical person, thus allowing him to be a pitcher, catcher, infielder, batter, and baserunner. A prospective baseball athlete might be evaluated for just one fielding position.

Patrick Cobb's Self-Evaluation of Junior Year Performance

1. *Pitching Skills*

    Objective measurements:
    - Record five wins, two losses
    - Innings pitched—42
    - ERA—3.04
    - Hits—26
    - Strikeouts—40
    - Bases on balls—30
    - Strikeout-to-walk ratio—4:3
    - Arm strength—78 m.p.h.
    (measured 5/19/85)

Subjective comments: Throws hard, but can be inconsistent at times. Fields the position well. Walks at critical times hurt.

Corrective action: Throw three times weekly during off-season and concentrate on accuracy.

Personal goals: Off-season—40 strikes in every 50 pitch practice
Season—strikeout-to-walk ratio—2.5:1

2. *Catching Skills*

Objective measurements:
- Threw out four of nine runners at second base
- Threw out seven of eight runners at third base
- Fielding percentage .975—two errors

Subjective comment: Good receiver, but does not have an exceptionally quick release to throw out runners.

Corrective action: Field 100 tennis balls off of a brick school wall and throw to second (or right back at the wall). Time action from the moment the ball is touched to the time the throw rehits the wall. Accuracy should not be sacrificed. Throw three times weekly during off-season.

Personal goals: To improve present fielding-throwing action an average of .2 seconds by the start of next season. Throw out 2/3 of all opponents' steal attempts to second base during next season.

3. *Fielding Skills*

Objective measurements:
- Fielding percentage—1.000

Subjective comments: Has limited fielding range, especially to his left. Sure hands, average arm. Great range and concentration on pop-ups.

Corrective action: Field 40 ground balls hit wide to player's left and 20 ground balls to player's right for 20 consecutive days during the off-season. Take a month break and repeat the skills for another 20-day period. Play another sport

| | stressing lateral movement to improve this skill. |
| Personal goals: | Play tennis actively. Improve ground ball fielding range even if it means sacrificing this year's perfect fielding percentage. |

4. *Batting Skills*

Objective measurements:	• Batting average—.331 • 12 RBIs in 61 at-bats • One double, one triple
Subjective comments:	Good bunter, hits to all fields, basically a line drive hitter.
Corrective action:	Improve strength to improve power statistics and RBI capability. Do 100 push-ups and 40 pull-ups daily.
Personal goals:	To have 10 extra base hits and 24 RBIs next season and show no degradation in batting average.

5. *Running Skills*

Objective measurements:	• Stole 14 bases in 16 attempts. 15.8 seconds from home-to-home after a hit.
Subjective comments:	Possesses good quickness and gets excellent "jump" on pitcher. Always uses headfirst slide.
Corrective action:	Spend ten practices in sandy area practicing hook slide and stand-up slide techniques.
Personal goals:	Improve home-to-home time by minimum of one full second. Use different slides during proper game situations. Achieve a 100 percent steal/attempts mark next season.

This hypothetical evaluation gives the reader a more direct approach toward skill improvements. It also creates an active corrective action program and includes the motivational factor (personal goal) needed for improvement.

Any type of evaluation can be made to fit your specific needs. Remember, objective evaluations include measurable marks like a basketball mark of 76 percent free throw accuracy, or a baseball statistic like a .331 batting average, or tennis measurement like 2.2 double-faults a match. Subjective evaluations are limited to comments like "good" free thrower, or "excellent" singles hitter, or "outstanding" server.

I will close this chapter by saying there is a great reward in measuring measurable statistics, because as you will see in the later stages of this book, there are opportunities to use the statistics to your advantage. The specific measurements can be used to market your skills, and that is what this book is all about.

Chapter III
The Six Areas of Improvement

It is my opinion that there are six basic areas in which an athlete should strive if he wants to raise performance levels in any sport or event. The six areas to concentrate on improving are (1) having goals, (2) solid knowledge of the sport in which you participate, (3) overall body strength, (4) basic skills and natural ability, (5) speed, and (6) sound academic background. Let's lay the groundwork for every reader by briefly discussing these important topics.

1. *Your goals.* As you read further into this chapter, think about the goals you have in mind for the future. What are your long-range plans? Plan your future with realistic personal goals, remembering that the bottom line in athletic endeavors is success. This success comes only from hard work. Since there is no easy way to stay above the level of competition in sports, you

must work extremely hard to achieve the goals you have set. If your ultimate goal is to win a college scholarship, the hard work represents the means to the end result.

Each athlete should establish short-term skill goals, intermediate performance goals, and seasonal goals. Even if your ultimate goal is a scholarship, you cannot chronologically advance any more than one season at a time. Year-by-year improvement may result in achievement of the ultimate scholarship goal; however, it is the shorter term goals which have immediate impact on your performance.

We will examine two athletes from two different sports specialities with the same ultimate goal of winning a college scholarship. Let's examine each athlete's different goals—each centered around each athlete's needs.

In a hypothetical example, Sally Thomas is a talented freshman tennis athlete who has been in competitive age-group tennis for six years. After competing as a freshman on the varsity team, Sally found that after observing her first school season's results, she never won a match which went into the third set, despite having a fine match record of seven wins and four defeats. Sally established her goals around being more effective in the final set. Sally decided to implement a plan which would help her for the next season's competition. Her short-term skill goal was to run a mile in a weighted jacket prior to and just after each practice session or match leading up to her sophomore season. Sally's intermediate goal was to play in three off-season tournaments which would virtually ensure three-set competition. Her seasonal goal for her sophomore year was to win every third-set match she played.

Ronnie Smith, in another hypothetical case, is a junior soccer player who has proven himself as a goaltender playing on a team which he led to a 12-3 won-lost mark and feels that his average of 1.2 goals per match was outstanding. He made marked improvement from his sophomore mark of 2.7 goals per match. Ronnie's goals for his upcoming senior season were established as follows: his short-term skill goal was to establish a rigorous agility/speed program which included regularly scheduled agilities that concentrated on improvement of vertical jumping ability and lateral quickness.

Ronnie established an intermediate goal for himself which was not agility/jumping related. He set out to measure his free kick distances and improve on his average kick by five yards per kick over his sophomore off-season marks. His senior season goals were to strive for a shutout in each match and average less than one goal per match. He felt that if he met his personal goals, his team would gain championship recognition and attract recruiters during season-ending statewide competition.

2. *Your knowledge of the sport.* You must have a thorough understanding of a sport if you wish to master it. And no one fully masters any sport without extensive knowledge of the activity. There are many different ways you can learn about your sport at very little expense to you. Probably the greatest sources of knowledge can be found in the school you attend, the library in your hometown, even in your own home. If you have the desire and interest, you will use these resources to your personal advantage.

Around your school you can learn many things. The greatest single source is your coach. He has spent a great many hours of his life either playing the game and/or preparing to teach your specialty. Ask him questions. Feel free to utilize his knowledge and his resources to better yourself. Chances are that the coach will let you borrow some of his sports magazines or coaching manuals. The coach also may have a complete library of printed materials that discusses your sport in infinite detail. The coach can also assist you by recommending and locating the better reading materials found in the school library. It is extremely advantageous for you to have a thorough knowledge of the most up-to-date rules. The coach should have a copy of the current rules in his office. You may also ask the coach for film on your sport so that you may study it. Film will allow you to critique yourself and/or other successful athletes.

To learn even more, go to the public library. Biographies and autobiographies of athletes and their personal experiences in the sport you play are usually good reading. Biographies also make you more aware of the challenges ahead as you advance to different levels of sports competition.

Your own subscription to a sports magazine can keep you

informed on the latest occurrences in the sports field. Also, television coverage of sports events has increased over the last few years. Watching a sports event on television can be a learning experience. You watch a golf tournament and lessons or rule interpretations are discussed. You watch a baseball game and the sports announcers analyze the possible tactics and strategies to be employed in certain situations as the game develops. Many times I have observed a game when the analyst, usually a former professional player or coach who understands the game, discusses and teaches fundamental skills. You may also see him comment to young players on what to do and what not to do in a certain sport situation.

There is a great deal to learn. Knowledge and awareness are *vital* to your success. Utilize the resources available to you. You can learn something new about your sport every day. Keep up with the latest techniques and learn more about the skills. The knowledge of skills and the knowledge of the sport allow you to improve the speed of your actions discussed later in this chapter.

3. *Overall body strength.* Probably the greatest single area of improvement found in athletes today can be found in the athlete's overall body strength. Athletes are stronger today because of advanced training techniques, progressive knowledge, and facilities available to athletes in the field of weight training.Many different philosophies exist concerning the form of weight training which is most beneficial. Each coach that you talk to will probably recommend a slightly different body development program. One coach may recommend free weights. Another coach may believe that an isometric contraction routine is the best method of training for you. Still another coach may utilize dynamic tension, but his chief competitor may believe in one use of weight lifting machines with many different exercise stations. Still another may believe in basic push-up–pull-up routines.

No matter what form of weight training facilities you may have at your access, or what form of strength development you decide is best for you, weight training should become a regular part of any athlete's training to prepare for a successful future. Young men lift weights. Young women lift weights. Athletes in every sport should include some form of strength improvement training in their workout routines. If you were to check on the most progressive athletic programs in the country, you would find that some form of weight lifting exercises is employed. Top basketball coaches recommend weights to improve speed, endurance and jumping ability. Baseball players lift weights to improve their throwing velocity, hitting power and overall speed. Track performers concentrate on weights to improve individual speed, jumping ability and overall body strength. Former Villanova all–American miler Marty Liquori lifted weights "to keep from being injured" in the long track season. Football players use weight training to increase strength, speed and bulk. If you want to know more about which weight lifting exercises can benefit you best, ask your coach. You may also receive a wealth of helpful information by writing or calling a college coach that you respect for his or her views on weight training in your sport.

Let me put weight training in perspective. If your goal is a college athletic scholarship, you must train not to be an outstanding high school participant, but you should train to become an outstanding collegiate participant.

But do not misunderstand. Both football players and swimmers will lift weights to get stronger, but they will not necessarily use the same methods to improve that strength. Some of the exercises may be the same in order to concentrate on similar muscle group improvement, but the amount of weight and number of repetitions will differ greatly. Each sport will be slightly different, so get some expert advice.

4. *Your basic skills.* Any higher level of competition requires more skills than the previous level did. You must improve your skills so that you can stay ahead of the competition. Let us look at a track performer who specializes in sprints. As a ten-year-old he wins the 100-yard dash in a fine time of 13.1 seconds in area competition to establish himself as the "fastest runner around." As he matures, he continues to improve his techniques of the start, and his pure speed improves through maturity. He wins junior high meets at 10.9 seconds. In high school the competition dictates that he continue to improve his time in order to achieve the

championship level to which he has grown accustomed. In the sprints, he must improve his time to 10 seconds flat prior to his senior year so that he can be highly competitive. Because he always works exceptionally hard to improve, he establishes consistent starts, a strong fluid stride, and an explosive finish. These skills allow him to surpass his goal of 10 seconds flat. He runs a 9.8! He has continued to improve because he has learned to combine his natural speed with the skills he has practiced in the 100-yard dash. He wins consistently. But he must continue to improve to be a competitive collegiate sprinter where competitive times are even lower.

This example of a sprinter tells a vivid story. In order to compete on the college level, athletes must improve their high school skills in a given sport. Successful performances depend on the athlete's ability to master these skills. The best athletes master their particular skills—sometimes referred to as fundamentals or techniques—by continual hard work and repetition.

The fundamentals can be learned. If you are an offensive lineman in football, you must learn to block, trap, pull and protect for the passer. If your specialty is infield play in baseball, you must learn to throw accurately and to field pop flies, grounders and line drives. If soccer is your game, you need to master the basics in heading, dribbling, tackling, shooting, etc. These examples are the fundamentals. The techniques associated with these athletes are the proper body angles used by the football lineman in executing specific blocks, or the footwork used by the infielder in executing the double play, or proper weight distribution and/or head placement by the soccer performer. When you master the techniques used in your sport, you will excel!

The fundamental skills include points previously mentioned in this chapter. Having knowledge of the skills and having the strength to endure constant practice and repetition are the key factors in developing the fundamentals. When you begin to master the skills, your performance will improve, your confidence will soar, and you will be eager to meet the challenge of the higher levels of competition ahead.

5. *Your speed.* Probably the most discussed skill in athletics today is speed. Webster's defines speed as "an act or state of mov-

ing rapidly; swiftness; quick motion." We almost always think of speed as quickness of foot, but this is not the only area to master. Athletic speed, to paraphrase Webster's definition, is the ability to move with swiftness and quick motion when performing the skills of your game.

If your specialty is throwing the shot put, your most important goal should be to develop the ability to get across the circle with speed. Your strength is vital, but your execution of techniques with speed across the circle is the skill that will bring you the greatest results and improvement.

You may be an excellent technician shooting the basketball, but the truly great player executes his shot with quickness. This speed allows him to shoot more uncontested shots, and this improves his field goal percentage.

Whatever your sport and whatever fundamental skills are required in your sport, you must constantly work to improve the rate of speed (combining the physical act with mental speed) at which you perform those skills. For all sports that have running involved, running speed is probably the most important single skill you can possess. Having the ability to beat out a base hit, or hit the hole faster for extra yardage, or execute the fast break for a lay-up are basic examples of what foot speed can do to make you a dominating player. But how do you improve your speed? The best way to get faster is to develop the running muscles through weight training, to isolate the skills of running (like practicing body lean and high knee action), and to practice running itself. You'll never get faster worrying about your speed. It is important for the athlete to practice the fundamentals of running like any other skill.

Before leaving our discussion of speed, I'd like to draw one more point. Having a thorough knowledge of your sport will help you to execute your skills faster. Anticipate the situations or problems that may confront you before the problems occur. Study the game and know the situations that could instantaneously occur. Many times in watching wrestling matches, I have seen an unaware grappler, with more ability than his opponent, lose a match at the buzzer because he did not execute a takedown fast enough. In most cases he lost because he did not know something as basic as the score of the match or because he was not aware of the time left in the match. If you know the situation, your speed and execution will be better because you have eliminated any doubt of what it takes to win!

6. *Your academic background.* The college athlete must be a very special person. I have discussed your personal goals. When you solidify your goals, be sure that you include the most enduring goal of all—your education. If you are awarded a college athletic scholarship, you will be a student at that college. You will be earning your way through college by utilizing your athletic skill. Your athletic talents and abilities are simply a means to the end—the college degree opportunity.

Many athletes become so engrossed in the athletic competition and preparation for the upcoming season that they simply ignore their academic responsibility. Do not wait until the last semester of your senior year of high school to prepare yourself for college. No outstanding student has ever lost the opportunity for an athletic scholarship because of good high school grades. But many, many good athletes have been denied the opportunity for an athletic grant-in-aid because of poor grades. Your education is what you make of it. As we discussed earlier, no athlete has ever gotten faster by worrying about his speed; he must work on that skill. The same is true of the student. No student ever improved his grades by ignoring his bookwork, homework, or course selection. Academic success should begin in the ninth grade; however, it is never too late to implement a "turnaround plan" for success.

Since there are some new guidelines which have recently been established by the National Collegiate Athletic Association, I strongly encourage you to become familiar with the chapter in this book called "Meeting Proposition 48 Guidelines." It discusses the specific courses and entrance requirements which have been established by the NCAA member institutions.

Whatever your grades or whatever your background in school, you must strive to improve your grades and to establish lasting study habits. Your grades will get you into college; your study habits will get you out of college with a degree.

Chapter IV

Where the Money
Comes From:
An Overview of
the Athletic Programs

The opportunity to win an athletic scholarship is a very rewarding and lucrative goal. The U.S. government does not subsidize its athletes in any way. The scholarship is the only way to reap the financial rewards and still maintain amateur status in American sports. And scholarships are available to both young men and young women in all sports. Let's take a look at the overall scope of an athletic administrator's view of the sports involved in an athletic program.

Revenue Sports

Naturally the greatest number of scholarships throughout the country are given in the revenue producing sports—the sports that generate income at each individual institution. Let's look at the economics involved. The revenue helps to pay the bills. The publicity enhances the image of the college. It has been speculated by media reports that Georgetown University officials estimated gross receipts of over $10 million to the University coffers which were indirectly attributable to the signing of high school basketball phenom Patrick Ewing. The university's enrollment increased, as did ticket sales, T-shirt sales, alumni endorsements, TV and radio receipts, NCAA play-off receipts, and so forth.

Opportunity to win an athletic scholarship is greatest in football and basketball. Fan interest, possibility of large TV contracts, gate receipts, and publicity are reasons that colleges place such a great emphasis on these sports. Football teams have large squads and generally attract large numbers of fans and alumni on Saturdays in the fall; therefore, a lot of money is made and a large number of scholarships is offered to deserving young athletes. Basketball in comparison has smaller numbers of players on each squad, but attracts large crowds in the winter months. Basketball teams play a greater number of games than football teams play. Each game can generate income.

What does this mean? If the budget of the program is greater, you can expect a greater emphasis on recruiting outstanding talent. There will therefore be more scholarships available. Hockey is played almost exclusively in cold weather areas of the country. Despite the geographical limitations of the game, hockey draws great crowds because it is a fast game with continued excitement. Great crowds—more money. That's right—more scholarships too! Track and field, wrestling, baseball, and swimming have proven to be revenue producing sports in different parts of the country.

Total Sports Program

But money is not the only criterion for a college or university to use scholarships to attract outstanding athletes. The second greatest reason for colleges to award scholarships is emphasis on a total athletic program. Many schools are committed to field competitive teams in each sport. This means they want to do well in every sport in which they field a team. Scholarship aid is thus appropriated to nonrevenue sports such as soccer, golf, tennis, baseball, softball, lacrosse, track and field, fencing, cross-country, volleyball, swimming, wrestling, skiing, gymnastics and more! Most of the major NCAA schools fall into this category. To place this emphasis on success in each sport, a college needs to subsidize each program to attract high calibre coaches and athletes in each sport. More emphasis and more scholarships.

The total athletic program usually transfers money generated from successful revenue producing sports programs into a budget to accommodate the sports which cannot generate funds of their own. This philosophy of well-rounded sports success usually lends itself to the college or university's overall philosophy of having its students experience well-rounded academic and social success. Oh, just one more thought: No one said that all donations from financially successful and interested alumni are from people interested in just football and basketball!

One-Sport Specialists

There is a third reason athletic scholarship aid is awarded to athletes by colleges or universities. Some colleges choose to put emphasis in one or two sports. Anyone interested enough to read this book is familiar with the emphasis school. The emphasis school specializes in one sport and tries to be excellent at just that sport. The emphasis school probably gives scholarship aid in that one sport and no others. It may participate in other sports, but only with nonscholarship athletes. The emphasis school is usually more common at the small college, private college (not state-supported), or the junior college levels. The sport selected for emphasis may be football, basketball, hockey, wrestling, baseball, tennis, swimming, skiing, gymnastics, golf or any other sport. To emphasize the chosen sport the college or university expands its budget and scholarship allotment in one of its athletic teams. Let's be basic. You are a college administrator. You do not want to run a program that costs you a lot of money, or even one that doesn't achieve successful results. Instead of trying to be average in many sports, you choose to emphasize one or two sports to bring recognition to your athletic program, give your alumni something to brag about, and help you to raise money in the general scholarship fund or athletic fund.

Let's say the sport you, the administrator, choose to emphasize is tennis. Your feelings are based on a strong alumni donation, or the limited cost of facilities, or the limited space available for sports facilities on your campus. Or maybe you are located in a geographical location which has excellent year-round weather to attract superathletes. You build new lighted tennis courts, and hire an ambitious coach with a successful teaching background to run your program. You instruct him to do whatever it takes within the rules to develop a program that will bring acclaim to the school.

The coach in turn goes to the high schools of America to find the best tennis players available. To locate the best talent available the coach watches high school matches, junior tennis tournaments, city recreational competition, and national tournaments. The coach also reads newspapers to follow up on results of competition he was unable to attend personally. After deciding which athletes he wants in this program, the coach begins to recruit talented young athletes whom he feels would be good for his program. The coach signs a few top players each year. He guides their emotional and academic progress, coaches them to master the tennis skills, and wins!

The tennis players whom the coach recruited have the opportunity to participate on the college level, have their education provided through a scholarship, graduate, and are happy.

The coach builds a lasting relationship with his players. He puts a representative team on the court. The tennis team brings acclaim to the college or university. Now the coach is happy.

You, the administrator, see fine young athletes play well enough to bring recognition to the college. You observe the young athletes progress toward graduation. You know that these young athletes will become helpful in future recruiting endeavors to keep the program growing. The acclaim won by the tennis team's accomplishments helps to unite the alumni to develop strong pride and interest in your college and its tennis program. The emphasis pays off, bringing publicity of excellence to the college. It generates emotional and financial support from friends of the college and alumni. The number of applications for admission to the college increases too! Now you, Mr. College President, are happy!

*   *   *

Where do you, the athlete, fit into the overall athletic picture? All throughout your high school career you have played hard to bring recognition to yourself, your family, your school. Your personal success is obvious. You have led your team in scoring; won all-state or all-county recognition or earned the captain's award for your individual leadership qualities. You love the sport. You have excelled. And you want to continue your athletic career. You'd like to someday become a professional athlete, but the most logical and sensible progression is for you to attend college and play a college sport. Both you and your parents want you to further your education. Even though they could help you to finance all or a portion of your college education, you want to do it on your own.

Since you have an athletic skill, a potential method of paying for your education exists. This method is to earn an athletic scholarship. You've heard scholarships mentioned before, but you're really not sure what scholarships are all about. You are aware that an athlete plays a sport in exchange for fees, books, tuition and/or meals, which gives the athlete a chance to earn a college education.

Your skills can earn you a scholarship. Your desire to improve your skills can earn you a scholarship. Ambitions and industriousness to find a college looking for your particular skill can earn you a scholarship. This skill, desire, ambition, and industriousness is what this book is all about: how you can earn an athletic scholarship and know what to look for after one has been offered to you.

Athletic teams are an important function of almost every college in America. Some place greater emphasis on sports than others, but almost every school fields teams to represent the school in intercollegiate competition. In most cases the capital outlay in each college athletic department around the country qualifies athletic programs as a big business. Do some simple figuring on your own. When the University of Michigan has 104,000 people at a football game six times a year, it does well financially. Add in profits from concessions, TV appearances, bowl games (a Rose Bowl bonanza!), and peripheral sales from clothing, etc., and you can quickly understand just how big a business football at the University of Michigan really is.

Here is why your skill can be qualified as a very precious commodity no matter how big or how small the school. After you decide on a college, your skills, blended with other talented performers from different parts of the country, come together to form a team. This team is molded together by a qualified coach or group of coaches. The coach and the team is the finished product. But to put that team on the field many expensive and important considerations must be handled. A look at the diagram of "College A" will help you to comprehend the scope of an athletic department. There are people who are employed to supervise your housing and to feed you. Still others are employed to account for athletic department expenses, transporting you from game to game, filming your efforts, and maintaining the locker rooms and fields. Employees responsible for distributing and cleaning equipment, selling tickets, teaching you in the classroom, tutoring you out of the classroom if necessary, administering the athletic department, and raising money all cost the institution money. Also, the services that all of these people provide cost a great deal of money.

Many dollars are spent on you, the athlete, so that you will have every opportunity to have a good playing career. If you

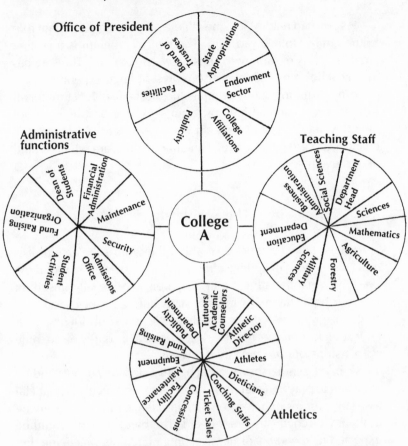

This pie chart example of College A shows two things. First, each athlete is only a small part of the overall athletic picture and an even smaller part of the university picture. Secondly, and conversely, the athlete has many people available to support his academic and athletic growth and development since the athlete contributes in a significant way to the university's overall publicity program.

perform well, chances are your team will win. When your team wins it generates fan and alumni enthusiasm. This enthusiasm generates ticket sales, booster club contributions, and publicity to the school. These sales, contributions, and publicity satisfy the needs of the school. Then, in turn, the sales and contributions help to pay for the expenses your team has incurred. Most basically it pays for your scholarship and your education.

As you can readily see, the athlete plays a very important role in the entire athletic program. The typical program is investing great amounts of money to subsidize scholarships. The services for the scholarship athletes also represent large expenditures.

Since winning teams generate the most effective return for all expenditures, each athletic program seeks the best high school talent available. If you have an exceptional athletic talent, the chances are great that there is an athletic program which would like to evaluate your skills.

The Scholarship

I have talked a great deal about the word *scholarship*. It is much used word in college circles, but in my travels in recruiting I've found that the athlete and his parents are usually unsure of what a scholarship really means. Many different types of scholar- ships, or *grants-in-aid,* are a college's way of subsidizing your education for services rendered. Let's look at a couple of example scholarships outside the athletic world.

A band scholarship would be awarded to an outstanding musician to play in a marching band. One who receives financial assistance for his or her excellence in science might be receiving a biology or chemistry grant-in-aid. The band student would be expected to spend his or her free time marching, practicing, lin- ing practice areas, or helping other band members at the school. The young science student may be asked to assist in lab studies, extracurricular science activities, or assist in scientific studies conducted by the college or university he attends. Thus, both the band student and the science student, who are both excellent in their respective interest fields, will be expected to render their particular services to the college in return for the grant-in-aid awarded to them.

The athletic grant-in-aid is similar to the band or science award just discussed. If you were to be awarded money for your abilities in a football skill, your ability is not the only service you offer the institution you agree to attend. As was said earlier, you will have your education subsidized for services rendered. In football your services will include living up to the team rules set by the coaches, attending team meetings, being in attendance at each practice session, making trips for games, and more. It will occupy a great deal of your free time. So, in signing a football grant, you will be agreeing to give the college your devoted efforts to the betterment of the football program. The same would be true in basketball. The same would be true in baseball or any other type of athletic grant-in-aid.

In summary, the scholarship or grant-in-aid is a college's way of paying you for your services rendered. It is not a free ride through college, but a way of earning your tuition, etc., in return for your competitive abilities.

Chapter V
Marketing the Athlete's Skills by Using the Five P's of Selling

Each college athletic staff offering scholarships will diligently explore each lead to locate the best available talent. Each staff, in turn, relies on a variety of sources for information to initiate the leads. The key element to meet the athlete's scholarship goals is to successfully attract attention to your talents. The failure to attract this attention will diminish the athlete's opportunity to win a scholarship to practically zero. By utilizing the methods discussed in this chapter you can successfully market your abilities, thereby attracting attention and garnering success.

Webster's describes a scholarship as "a specific gift of money or other aid, as by an institution to help a student continue his studies." "Marketability," says Webster's, is "the quality or condition of being marketable."

An athlete's marketability has a direct effect on the dollar value of any scholarship awarded. Since effective selling skills and proper marketing strategy are discussed in great detail in this chapter, it is very important that the reader pay close attention to the material presented. Since a full athletic scholarship can be valued at $20,000 to $60,000 over a four year period (depending on various locations and institution fees assessed), it is important information.

This discussion will include techniques and examples of effective methods to be employed by each of the important people involved in the marketing process. The most important item to remember in the goal at hand is to successfully market your skills, accomplishments, and abilities into scholarship aid. The athlete should follow some basic sales principles which will create more effective salesmanship and eliminate some gray areas when interfacing with the college recruiter. It is for this reason that I have included this discussion of the "Five P's of Selling." The successful salesperson is the one who "dots all of the i's and crossess all of the t's." The athlete should coordinate his sales efforts with his coach in order to enhance uniformity in the sales effort. This effort, and coordination of the effort will be the finished product.

1. *Preparation.* Because the college recruiter is limited in the amount of time he can spend at any particular high school, it is essential that you and your high school coach prepare a factual résumé of your athletic and academic accomplishments. The résumé should include important items such as recommendations, academic progress and college board test results. Your efforts in preparing this information, which should be mimeographed for multiple-recruiter use, will provide the recruiter with some quantifiable facts which will help him to make some important decisions regarding your future. This profile, coupled with some preselected film or videotape playing highlights (only five to ten minutes' worth), is all that is needed to stimulate an interest in your behalf. The résumé and the film selection should be done *prior to* a recruiter's visitation.

Since a recruiter will more than likely visit the school during classroom hours, it is important that you coordinate your "preparation" with your coach so that he always has your résumé and film on hand in his office.

I suggest that you make as many as 50 photocopies or mimeographed copies of the résumé and keep them on file. The organized, mimeographed form can be used and re-used successfully to provide prompt, accurate and pertinent information each time you and/or your high school coach are contacted. It can also be used each time your high school coach wants to contact a college coaching staff. I strongly suggest that you have your high school coach include a copy of this important information along with any correspondence to a college regarding your performance and capabilities. Your coach can also staple it to guaranteed postage cards sent by colleges or along with requested questionnaire-type inquiries. Your efforts to finalize this information will be rewarded, since this profile can also be utilized as a form of guideline reference material for recruiters who call for information about you.

As a recruiter I always appreciated a copy of this type of mimeographed form to be included in any film transaction, too! Remember, you make the recruiting job easier by including pertinent data, like SAT scores, jersey numbers and career highlights. Remember, it is your responsibility to coordinate the effort to sell your abilities and market your strengths, since you are the one who will benefit.

One effective idea which always impressed me was to prepare a loose-leaf binder with the résumé, a picture and the academic profile. Your efforts to help prepare this information, combined with those of any teammates with similar aspirations, can help to win collegiate attention. The résumé, picture and academic record can be encased in a clear plastic holder. This method would not only impress the recruiter about you, but also about your coach, too, as an organized thinker. It helps to make a good impression for all concerned, as well as to help the recruiter better utilize his time effectively. Your preparation will help to get you the look that you want. The saying "don't put off for tomorrow what can be done today" is especially important for the junior and senior athletes. "Be prepared" is not limited to only the Boy Scouts of America.

2. *Pride*. After reviewing your résumé and your 5- or 10-minute film clip, the recruiter must make his first decision: Does he want to meet you? If the answer is "no," that's OK because you succeeded in having him evaluate your performance. If the answer is "yes, I'd like to meet the athlete," you're already into "Round 2." It is in Round 2 that the recruiter creates his most important impression: What does he think of you?

Would you like to hear some professionally negative tip-offs? Apathy. Arrogance. Lack of confidence. Dull. Unkempt. All negatives. Remember, you've already passed "Round 1."

Would you like to know some positive responses? Simple things like a firm handshake. A look into the recruiter's eyes, not at his shoes. Good grooming—which means clean-shaven boys—and clean clothes. And a quiet confidence that you are a good enough player to compete at the recruiter's school. Be a better listener than you are a talker, since it is the recruiter's job to interest you toward his program in "Round 2." The most impressionable thing I could recommend to all athletes, when meeting the recruiter, is to show him or her your deepest respect. If you do this, you'll make a favorable impression and provide the pride and self-confidence factors which you are being evaluated for in this interview.

3. *Probing the recruiter*. What does the recruiter really think about the athlete's talents? Many times you and your high school coach assume that each recruiter feels the same positive way about an athlete's potential as a student-athlete. Do not isolate your conversation from your coach. Compare notes! The successful sale includes the ability to make the recruiter declare his interest level. Asking questions will eliminate false hopes and allow you and your high school coach more time to spend with the recruiters who demonstrate a more sincere level of interest in your potential as a future athlete playing in their program.

Some of the simplest questions, or probes, will force the recruiter to not only tell you of his feelings about your performance, but will also keep the recruiter from creating a false impression at any point in the recruiting process. The probes should be straightforward and require definitive answers. You and your coach should know:

- Do you qualify academically? If not, what is required?
- Do you qualify athletically (height, weight, speed, skill)?
- Have you formally been offered a scholarship? If so, what is its value?
- Is the scholarship offer contingent on any specific parameters?
- If you haven't been offered a scholarship, when can you expect a decision?
- What position are you being recruited to play at College X?
- Are all academic programs at College X available to you?

Probing can clear up many doubts in a hurry, and keep you from being misled. Do not assume that if the recruiter is ever-present, that the athlete is locked into a situation. Continue to probe the recruiter throughout the recruiting process in order to learn if there is a change. Yogi Berra's "it ain't over 'til it's over" applies to you until the day you sign on the dotted line.

4. *Pep/enthusiasm.* The athlete whose actions demonstrate the qualities expected of a successful athlete will many times impress the recruiter. An outward demonstration of enthusiasm and sincerity will usually help the scholarship candidate. A positive impression often gets the recruiter to return for a second look even if the recruiter is not "sold" the first time around. Enthusiasm is a very important, contagious intangible that no one can measure in the sales transaction. And it does do a lot for your chances when you demonstrate an enthusiasm for the game when you're playing it on the field. The closest vocabulary word to enthusiasm I know is "hustle."

5. *Persistence.* As this discussion regarding the athlete's ability to sell himself in the recruiting process continues, it is important that we single out an example of the fifth "P" — persistence, or stick-to-itiveness. The athlete who understands the recruiting process will never stop selling his finished product. And recruiters admire persistence. Persistence wears down resistance, especially after successful probing declares an accurate assessment of a specific college's interest level. You must follow up on the progress which is being made by anticipating the next step in

the recruiting process. The athlete who coordinates his efforts with his coach by practicing persistence can have a very positive influence in the athlete's placement into a college scholarship program. The recruiting process can remind one of a maze with many dead-end passages, and at times it will become an extremely frustrating experience—for you and your coach. It is important that you don't alienate your coach or your recruiter, but help each of them. Your high school coach will make a gallant attempt to sell your athletic abilities to all recruiters during the normal recruiting period (which is different for each sport). A typical scenario finds that the coach "came close" on a couple of occasions, but the interested college recruiters opted to offer scholarships to other athletes at other high schools. Let's examine a typical example of persistence paying off:

After the decision was made not to offer a scholarship to Joey B., the recruiter informed the high school coach that Joey B. was "*almost* good enough" to offer a scholarship, but felt his college could not recruit him *at that time*. The persistent salesperson stores this conversation in his memory bank for the time that is the "right time." The key facts of the conversation are that Joey B. was "almost" there.

There have been many examples during my recruiting experiences where an athlete such as Joey B. and his coach who continued to sell his abilities were ultimately successful because the follow-up attempt to resell Joey B. came with good timing. Timing is a very key element which opens opportunities to young men and women. Many athletes are awarded scholarship money each year because the athlete and his interested, professional high school coach, who believed in a certain young athlete, gave second and third efforts to generate greater interest in the athlete. Let me explain why this ever-so-frequent event occurs.

Each year every collegiate coaching staff in America sets lofty goals to recruit high school athletes who will perform with greater efficiency than those presently in their program. Efficiency may come in the form of more athletic talent or in the form of smarter, more poised athletes. "If we are to improve as a team, we must recruit better athletes at each position" is the college coaching staff's motto. Of course, this motto is very idealistic. The outset of every recruiting season begins with this "better" philosophy. As the recruiting year continues, however, the staff must face the reality that "there are only a select number of better-quality athletes this year." If each college could meet its "better" goal, there would be many, many teams vying for the national championship. As the recruiting year gets closer to the signing date deadline, the top prospects begin to cast their commitments with many different institutions. College staffs, who have attempted to hold scholarship money for the "blue chip" athlete who commits to a rival school, suddenly begin to look at blank spaces on their recruiting lists. The scramble to fill those blank spots with the best available talent begins all over again. It is with this thought in mind that this publication can prove to be extremely helpful. Remember, an athlete with one full scholarship will ultimately prove to have the same financial reward as the athlete with twenty offers, because each can only commit to one school.

The athlete or his high school coach should never feel awkward when attempting to contact a college for a second or third time if there is a deserving, unplaced athlete who can compete in that institution's competitive environment. Let's expand why the second and third efforts could prove to be helpful to the deserving athlete without a scholarship.

Persistence is a very key element, because you and your coach should understand that there are four desirable times for a high school coach to expose, market and sell his athlete's talents. The first attempt should be made by recommending the athlete prior to the senior sport season. This early recommendation will give the athlete an opportunity to be observed by the college staff by means of film evaluation, practice observation, or game performances. The exposure gained prior to your senior season allows college recruiting staffs to plan effectively—possibly to observe you at the same time they evaluate an opposing player on your schedule. Remember that the best recruiting environment is created by those prospects and their coaches who make the recruiter's job easiest.

The second best time to market the athlete is during the senior season or just after the senior season. This is clearly the most common time for recommendation.

The third most opportunistic time to sell the athlete's abilities is by contacting specific institutions' staff members just prior to or just after announced conference-affiliated signing dates or national association signing dates. A probing follow-up during the signing date period will usually find many college coaches/recruiters searching for new talent to add to their recruiting boards. During this time you and your coach should make a personal telephone call to prospective College X, because the caller will receive a strong signal of the college's needs at that point in the recruiting season. I have found in my experiences that, during the signing date period, the high school coach many times finds an exhausted coaching staff which is very vulnerable for a positive solution to fill voids on its recruiting board created by high schoolers who chose to participate at a rival institution.

The fourth best time to sell the athlete is during late summer, even as late as a pre–school year coaching clinic, when every high school is concentrating their efforts on "next year." Many times a college coaching staff, in an attempt to fulfill its initial goal of signing "better" athletes, may have offered scholarship money to one or two "academic risks" or questionable students—athletes with marginal-to-poor high school academic records and grades. Then the institution's admissions office officially denies the athlete acceptance to the offering institution, and the scholarship offer is withdrawn, causing a scholarship to become available. The most outstanding part of the late-summer follow-up is that if scholarship money is available, there are very few uncommitted, quality student-athletes who are still available to be signed to a scholarship. Although one may find a limited number of academic risk–type scholarships which have become available, the competition at year's end is scanty. This is a great time to sell a good athlete who has recently experienced a late growth spurt or has proven two-sport ability.

The recruiting process never stops. Proper timing and persistence can be the means to the end. The "never-say-die" locker room slogan may be the message of one deserving athlete to his or her coach. I have prepared a résumé checklist of important ideas to help you search for scholarship aid (see Appendix A). They can serve as a checklist for pertinent information.

Chapter VI
"The Helping Hands"

The thrust of this chapter is to remind the reader that the institution awarding the scholarship learns about an athlete's ability in many different ways. The material presented in this chapter probably represents the most helpful information offered in this publication, because it is the area which is most often neglected by the candidate and those interested in promoting the candidate's skills. There is no set formula for success; therefore, the reader will be made aware of the many different interested people who can become involved in stimulating an interest level in the athlete. These people are the first type of "Helping Hands."

Each year a large number of deserving athletes lose their opportunity for scholarship aid because there is no ability to produce substantial evidence to support the college's interest. An athlete with the ability to play collegiately can prove his or her athletic skills by successfully marketing their skills. The devices employed by the athlete to accomplish this goal are the second type of "Helping Hand."

To gain the proper attention, each person involved must sell the athlete's accomplishments, achievements and leadership abilities. But most importantly, the helping hands must be able to support the claims made in behalf of the athlete. Each helping hand must fully understand his role and responsibility to successfully market the deserving candidate. Any of the following methods can be effective:

Helping Hand #1—The High School Coach

The high school coach says about a prized athlete, "I give up! I just don't know what the colleges want in an athlete. Joey can play college ball." Oh, I would like to have been paid one dollar for each time I heard a statement similar to that type of statement. The high school coach gets frustrated in his attempt to help land a scholarship award for the young athlete who has made outstanding contributions to his program during the past few seasons. My advice to the coach is to do exactly what he teaches his players to do—to keep trying; to practice persistence.

The coach must learn to take off his coaching hat and wear his salesman's hat when he attempts to sell his prospect's abilities and accomplishments. As a recruiter, I always liked to think that the player somewhat reflected the image of his head coach. If the coach was uninterested in helping me in my recruiting efforts, I felt that possibly there was a somewhat limited interest in the future of his athletes. The interested and dedicated coach usually leads the recruiter to an interested and dedicated athlete. The athlete who communicates with his coach during the recruiting process can help his own cause. The athlete who can continue to sell himself will continue to get the coach's attention and efforts to aid the cause.

Helping Hand #2—The Athlete and His Family

• "My favorite school hasn't contacted me. How can I get them interested in my talents?"

• "Because of our remote, rural location my high school never has college recruiters come by to visit with our athletes. What can I do to be noticed?"

• "The only colleges that visit our school are local institutions. How can I get a college from another geographical region to come by and take a look at me?"

• "The best lacrosse program in the country is in New York. How can I get that college to recruit me from Colorado?"

• "None of the colleges in my area has offered me a scholarship. Is my playing career over? Should I give up the search?"

Each of these questions is both common and logical. Each question deals with a slightly different level of frustration. Each asks how a talented athletic individual can attempt to sell his skills for scholarship money. Here's how you and your family can go scholarship hunting.

An athlete and his family must keep in mind three basic steps in order to successfully sell the son's or daughter's skills to a college or university. The first step is to locate the colleges who offer grants-in-aid in the athlete's sport. The second step is to properly contact the college in a formal manner. The third, and most important, step is to practice persistence and follow up on each lead. Let's take a closer look at each step in greater depth:

*Step 1—Locating the Colleges Offering
Grants-in-Aid in the Athlete*

With the exposure from large, national newspapers, magazines and television networks, an interested family can readily identify the many colleges which play specific sports. It appears that increasing recognition and exposure is given to minor sports, too! Let me give a few basic ideas as to how the family can locate potential colleges. The key factor is to utilize all the different forms of information available. Begin the search by utilizing the newspaper coverage. The interested family has the opportunity to read its local newspaper, which probably has coverage of the college results in the reading area. The family can find that larger metropolitan area newspapers usually include a greater regional coverage or even a national rundown of scores and results which occur in the specific sports season. But newspapers are not the only means in helping a family gather information as to which colleges play which sports. Radio or television coverage can help identify participants.

Let's get very basic and say that you don't have any print, TV or radio exposure. All you need to know is the name of one college participating in the specific sport in which you are interested. After identifying, you can call or write for a schedule of matches or games. The schedule will create a multitude of potential, since all the colleges on that schedule field teams, too! To build on this schedule thought process, a family can contact the other members of the schedule for their team schedule, which will soon become a national network of participants.

If you don't choose to employ either method previously stated, the family can simply create a knowledge base by probing neighbors who attended various colleges, professional contacts, and the teaching or coaching staff regarding whether each mentioned college has a competitive team in a given sport. The guidance counselor at the high school can possess a wealth of literature and information if a family is experiencing difficulty in locating colleges which participate in a lesser-played sport like fencing or gymnastics. It may take some effort, but no family should be isolated from opportunity if the will to succeed persists.

Probably the greatest source of information and knowledge sought by family members is the prospective athlete's high school coach. Chances are that the coach either played the sport which he coaches or is very interested and aware of the colleges who have intercollegiate programs. Assistant coaches can be helping hands, too. The athlete and his family can also utilize information provided by former high school teammates who have left the local high school to participate in a college sports program. Ask the former athletes about the schools they attend, the number of scholarships available, as well as the opponents on their team schedules. Before too much time has elapsed, I'm confident that the members of the athlete's family will find many, many leads regarding intercollegiate scholarship programs. If the family is not satisfied with its personal survey, I would recommend that a family member purchase the *1987 Blue Book for Senior College Athletics,* edited by A. W. Tinker, copyrighted and published by The Rohrich Corporation, 903 East Tallmadge Avenue, Akron, Ohio, 44310, $12.00. Also available from the Rohrich Corporation is the *1987 Blue Book of Junior College Athletics,* $11.00. These two publications will be consolidated into the *1988 Blue Book for Senior, Junior and Community College Athletics* and will sell for $15.00 each. The telephone number of the Rohrich Corporation is 216-659-3923. Each of *the Blue Books* is an excellent, updated source for researching collegiate athletic programs from each state in the country. *The Blue Book* includes addresses, phone numbers, coaches' names, conference affiliations, association membership (like the NCAA), and more. *The Blue Book* will leave no stone unturned in aiding the family's search to locate every four year intercollegiate program in every sport played.

Step II—Contacting the College

The first contact with a college head coach or recruiter should be executed by drafting a letter and personal data sheet. Any such contact should be done in a very neat and concise way. Remember that a family's efforts must concentrate on the task at hand—to sell the athlete's talents in exchange for a grant-in-aid. Be very neat (I suggest typed correspondence) so that the request can be easily read. Be concise so that your request can be easily understood.

In my experiences as a recruiting coordinator for a major college football program, I have received letters and calls from thousands of players, coaches and family members from each geographic region of the country. Many of the first contact letters I received from students went right into the wastebasket! Why? Because the student writer created a first impression of an ex-

treme level of incompetence or lack of ability to successfully
compete in the academic environment. Many other letters
created doubts. Many letters from students have been without
complete sentences or overloaded with misspelled words. Please
remember, athletic enthusiasts, that colleges are institutions for
higher education. With this thought in mind, the athlete should
demonstrate his ability to do college-level academic work in his
letter as well as sell his abilities as an athlete. And the athlete
should be the family member directing the correspondence. The
"proud papa syndrome" can become a tactical liability. It is my
opinion that fathers and mothers are better in the role of advisors
in the recruiting process rather than doers of the recruiting process. Your family should channel its efforts through you. The
athlete should be allowed to be the family representative because
it is his efforts which are to be sold. Feature the athlete and his
abilities as a successful student and athlete. Feature an athlete
who can demonstrate maturity and ambition. OK, athletes, are
we ready to write that introductory letter?

Be concise. Get your point across. Don't attempt to "flower-
up" the introductory letter. Here's why. When an athlete attempts
to flower-up the basic requests, the effort takes on a desperate
sound. Let me demonstrate an example of the most common
passage written by athletes in an introductory letter to secure an
athletic scholarship:

Dear Head Coach of College T:

I like your school. It is where I want to go to college. Do you have any
scholarships? I need one in order to attend college.

Sincerely,
Joey Brown

Let's analyze this typical letter before we actually get down
to the task at hand. The first statement was "I like your school."
The recruiter knew that Joey liked the school to some degree
when he opened his letter. If Joey didn't have an interest in College T he would not have written. A more dignified approach
might read, "I am impressed with your strong basketball program
and its commitment to excellence."

In the second sentence Joey stated, "It is where I want to go to college." Joey stated emphatically that College T is his first and only choice. A prospective student athlete should not comment regarding his ultimate intentions, no matter how strong his or her feelings may be. Remember that your purpose for writing is for financial assistance and that you are initiating a negotiation of sorts. The negotiation involves the university's money in fair exchange for your performance capabilities. Perhaps the recruiter reading the letter may feel that Joey would probably attend College T whether the athletic program offered scholarship money or not. A more discreet method may be to write, "Because of the strong forestry program, I am interested in College T."

Joey's question, "Do you have any scholarships?" is vague and not very specific. Remember, an athlete is interested in a scholarship for his services for playing in a specific sport—not financial aid, which is available to all students based on family income status. Joey's letter may have been read initially by a secretary or recruiter for all sports. Again, get the basic point across. You might write a statement like, "If College T offers grants-in-aid for basketball, please check my credentials on the following page or contact my coach for a recommendation. I feel that I am qualified to compete in your program." Remember that you are selling your abilities.

Joey's last statement of, "I need a scholarship to go to college" may be the most sincere statement written; however, it may also be the most wasteful statement made in the example letter. The college recruiter or coach may have felt some compassion for Joey's needs, but it is within his sports program's charter to locate the very best athletes available. The college recruiter will want to know about your high school performance and accomplishments long before he gets interested in your personal needs. No college program in any sport invests their scholarship money without having a high confidence level that the scholarship athlete will bring a strong return for that investment.

Now let's look at a letter which is both effective and concise. Do not hesitate to use this letter for your personal advantage. The only successful letter is one which gets results. We will also examine an example of a "homemade" personal data sheet which should be included on a separate page with your letter of inquiry.

200 Park Avenue
Union, SC 23279
June 1, 1985

Mr. Richard Jones
Head Track & Field Coach
College S
Collegetown, USA

Dear Coach:

I am presently a rising senior at Union High School. My coach has informed me about your strong track program and its commitment to
excellence.

I am interested in College S because of its track program as well as its
excellent reputation in business administration.

If College S offers grants-in-aid in track, please check my credentials on
the attached page or contact my coach for a recommendation. I feel that
my accomplishments qualify me to compete successfully in your
program.

Should you feel that my accomplishments are as impressive as those
marks set by the athletes now competing at College S, please mail me
some printed material about your track and field program.

Sincerely,
Joey Smith

Personal Data Sheet

Name: Joey Smith   School: Union (S.C.) High School
        200 Park Avenue   Route 9
        Union, SC 23279   Union, SC 23279
        803-427-7708   803-247-1000

Track Event	Best Distance/Time	Date
Long jump	22'11"	3-28-83
Triple jump	46'½"	5-12-83
100-yard dash	9.9 seconds	4-17-83

Personal Data:
        Height: 5'10½" (measured 5-19-83)
        Weight: 161 lbs. (5-19-83)
        Grade Point Average: 3.15 through six semesters
        SAT Scores: Verbal 410, Math 490 (4-19-83)
                      plan to retake test in November 1983

Track Awards:
        1st place Bearcat Relays Triple Jump
        All-county–long jump 1982, 1983
        All-conference–long jump 1983

<u>Track Coach:</u> Mr. Jim Brown 803-427-1000
                 Practice session videotape film is available upon request (jersey #14)
<u>Other Sports:</u> Basketball (Coach Richardson)
                 Point guard—jersey #22

Senior Year Track Schedule

3-15 at Smith	4-12 at Millburn
3-17 at Madison	4-17 Denton
3-21 at Bearcat Relays	4-28 County meet at Denton
4-1 Razorback Invitational	5-24 State Qualification
4-5 Clancy	

The introductory letter and data sheet give a college recruiter all the information he needs in order to cultivate an interest and follow up on the inquiry. After the coach/recruiter reads both the letter and the data sheet, the athlete will get his first feedback. Joey asked for printed material if his accomplishments "are as impressive as those marks set by the athletes now competing at College S." He will get a positive reinforcement if he receives literature. By receiving the materials he will be better informed by knowing (1) more about his abilities in comparison with the current athletes in the track program at College S, (2) more about the College S track program and its former athletes, and (3) that he should follow up on the inquiry at a later date.

If Joey does not receive literature, he should channel his efforts toward another college or redirect a similar correspondence at a later date. Why the later date? Let's discuss the follow-up techniques.

Step III—The Follow-up

Follow up only with the individual sports programs which have demonstrated an interest in the athlete. The athlete and his family must act on a timely basis to ensure that each institution continues to have the athlete's credentials in mind. What is "a timely basis"? A timely basis will vary with each contact which is made. It is a period of time which clearly allows the college coaching staff sufficient time to react to the recruiting action. Remember the discussion in the "persistence" portion of the

"Five P's of Selling" section of this book. In that section is defined the four most desirable times to be recruited. Look at the following negative example of being too hasty. Keep in mind that you are attempting to sell your abilities, not give them away.

Nothing irks a busy recruiter more than an overly persistent young athlete who oversells his interest. Don't call the recruiter one day after mailing him a letter or film. Don't take the recruiter's schedule for granted and expect him to review your film one hour after receiving it. Allow a reasonable amount of time to elapse before getting itchy.

On the contrary, the athlete should continue his follow-up with the colleges who have demonstrated an interest in his abilities. He should eliminate his childhood dream of attending "dear ole College M" and concentrate on solid leads. Getting offers for scholarship participation must remain the foremost goal. The opportunity to decide on the best one will come later in the recruiting process. Firstly, find out which schools want you to play for them. Secondly, the athlete should decide what is best for him.

More often than not an athlete will let his or her emotional ties dictate the scholarship hunting efforts. The athlete should continue to seek as many chances to be observed and gain as much exposure to scholarship programs as time allows, since there will be periods of time which tend to make the recruiting process come to a quick end. Be persistent. Somewhere there is a college looking for a quality athlete to bolster its program. Remember the "one full scholarship is equal to twenty scholarships" comment made earlier. Keep plugging; you only need one to reach your goal. The second and third offers allow you the luxury of making a choice.

The most effective method of follow-up is to utilize an updated personal data sheet. All pertinent information which changes (for the better) should be included and become a sales tool for the athlete. Maybe he improved his SAT test score, or he improved his best time in the 100-meter breaststroke. Let it be known. Notify your coach, mail an update, or telephone the recruiter of the improvement in your status.

The athlete who works closely with his high school coach

will get the best follow-up results. Let the coach make the contact to update the accomplishment. Allow the coach to act as your agent.

Sometimes an athlete doesn't choose to work closely with the high school coach. Lack of a successful relationship with a high school coach can virtually put the nails in the athlete's coffin; however, scholarship success has sometimes been achieved. Possibly the high school coach has become discouraged with his failure to help the athlete. The possibility exists that a coach may have a limited idea of an athlete's long-term potential. If the coach's discouragement is the reason, let me suggest that the athlete and his family member thank the coach for his efforts and ask to borrow some of the better game films or videotapes to be mailed independently of the coach's efforts.

One more tip to the athlete's family efforts. Anticipate your needs before your senior season. When an athlete is considering college institutions outside his immediate statewide area, it is imperative to produce filmed evidence of the athlete's talents. The film and/or videotape makes a geographically isolated (rural, inner-city) and underpublicized athlete an equal opportunity athlete. If the school does not take film, I strongly suggest that before the outset of the senior season the athlete and his family find some interested booster or fan to take home movies of games, practices or scrimmages.

Anticipate the problems of marketing your athletic abilities. Work with the high school coach. Continue to update the personal data sheet. Follow up on the interested colleges. Get offers. Follow up, follow up, follow up ...

Helping Hand #3 — Film as a Visual Aid

Let's talk about the utilization of film. I have mentioned it many times. One of the truly great teaching aids in sports today is film. Putting aside its obvious coaching/teaching/strategy advantages, film may prove to be the best tool to demonstrate and prove your talent level. It can capture a stellar performance which may not be observed in person. During my recruiting experiences, I have viewed hundreds of high school game films in a variety of forms. Sixteen millimeter, eight millimeter, and videotape cartridges are clearly the most common forms.

Ask your booster organization to raise the money for film if your school doesn't film. No film can mean no visible proof of your playing. Film as a teaching aid will help your coaching staff to improve the intricacies of the athletic performance. Film as a concrete proof of athletic performance will help place you and other athletes into college programs. Any coach who is operating within a limited budget environment will not be able to afford the luxury of film. If this is the case, let me suggest to the coach with a limited budget that he utilize his options within his community. You or your coach can ask some interested parent, fan or booster to use, rent, or borrow a home movie outfit to film one or two practices or events. Five minutes of film is better than none at all. Although the home movie–type film is not likely to be of professional quality, it does provide a tangible opportunity for a college coach to expand his or her capabilities to evaluate an athletic prospect. A film taken in Maine for the purpose of selling a prospect's abilities is equally effective in Florida or Texas. A rural or inner-city athlete can be seen just as readily as the athlete who performs in a more highly recruited metropolitan area. Film captures the performance and gives your athlete an equal opportunity to be measured and evaluated.

Before stopping the important discussion regarding filming of any athletic event, I will include one suggestion to those novice coaches or novice readers who choose to employ the home movie method of filming. My one suggestion is to film from the highest available vantage point. If you film football, have the photographer position his camera in the press box or upper stands. If swimming or baseball is the event, film a meet or game from a vantage point which has elevated the camera angle. Any gymnasium event like wrestling or basketball should be filmed from the upper levels of the bleacher area.

My experience tells me to remind you that film can get lost. Mark the school's name on each piece of film which is mailed. Each time you or your coach distributes the film for evaluation, be certain to record which film(s) have been sent to College X.

Also, record the date the film was mailed, delivered or picked up by a recruiter. Time is one of the biggest opponents a prospect or coach faces in searching for an interested college. Make sure to have the college who is borrowing the film know you expect its return in a reasonable amount of time. The expectation of the recruiter returning the film on time is a professional courtesy which should be met by the borrower.

It is a timesaving practice to never allow any film to be sent without including the prospect's uniform number and jersey color worn during the filmed event. There may be two #65s playing right guard. Swimmers or track performers who do not have jersey numbers should make it clear which designated lane the athlete performed in. The recruiter or coach who requests the film may not be the person who will evaluate the film. Leave no doubts about which athlete is to be evaluated.

In summary, film can certainly play an important role in placing the athlete in college. It is of the utmost importance to provide visual aids from the athlete's high school to any college athletic program in the country. Film and a pertinent information data sheet offer these visual communications. Whoever said that "one picture is worth more than ten thousand words" might have been talking about marketing a young athlete's skills to earn a college athletic scholarship.

Helping Hand #4—The College Alumnus in the Community

If an alumnus of College M has had the opportunity to notice a talented athlete in his community, he should not hesitate to make the coaching staff at College M aware of the athlete's accomplishments. This form of assistance is practiced by college alumni and interested friends of college institutions all over the country. Many quality athletes remain unnoticed by recruiters because they play nonglorified positions in team sports or participate in programs without the benefit of media coverage. The greatest example of an unnoticed athlete comes in the form of a talented player who plays on the same team with a "superstar" who receives all the rave notices. I have witnessed many second-best players who have gone to colleges as walk-ons and had better college careers than their former teammates who were highly recruited.

On the other hand, an alumnus should never assume that each star athlete is being recruited by his college. An alumni contact allows greater depth in the college's recruiting efforts. Let's discuss some helpful timesaving tips for the alumnus who wants to become involved in the recruiting process to help his institution.

If an alumnus contacts the college coaching staff by letter, it might be helpful to include a newspaper article or picture about the athlete's performance. The news clip can serve as a means to "justify" the alumnus' opinion.

Should the alumnus choose to contact the college coaching staff by telephone, he should be prepared to offer some additional data to expedite the college staff's recruiting efforts. Before calling, especially if your college is out-of-state, try to jot down the high school coach's name and telephone number as well as the athlete's name and phone number.

An alumnus' effort may prove to be helpful to his alma mater. More importantly, however, it may create an opportunity for a deserving local athlete to win a grant-in-aid. When the alumnus observes an athlete whose achievements have not received a great deal of recognition, he should not let that fact discourage his effort to help. Quality alumni recommendations can also help to reduce the college's overall recruiting expenses.

One very important note: An alumnus should contact the coaching staff or recruiter *prior* to any personal discussions with the athlete or his family. The rules restrict personal alumni contacts. Please ask for direction before contacting the athlete so that the athlete's scholarship eligibility will not be jeopardized. Recruiting rules protect the personal privacy of the recruited athlete. A personal contact by alumni could become "foul play" in the recruiting process. May I repeat: *Work with and through the college coaching staff.* Remember, the alumnus should become informed of the latest recruiting regulations by asking questions of the college staff. Yes, an alumnus can become a strong helping hand to both the local athlete and the college recruiter.

Helping Hand #5—Using a Tryout to Demonstrate Your Skills

When all other forms fail, there is one reliable method to attract a coach to notice your abilities: the tryout. A tryout is a physical test given by a college coaching staff on the college's premises to evaluate the basic skill level or ability level of individual athletes. The tryout represents a bona fide opportunity for any athlete to demonstrate his talent. Since each college coaching staff may use a different group of measurements, it is important that we discuss some examples of what a tryout entails.

One college may be most concerned with analyzing specific mechanical skills which are directly related to the sport in which you play. Examples of specific skills which might be evaluated in a tryout might be serving or volleying techniques used in tennis or volleyball, or batting skills or pitching skills in baseball. Another vivid example of a specific skills-type tryout is to have a golf prospect play a round of golf with the coach. During the round the coach can observe putting skills, sand trap capability and driving accuracy.

Another tryout approach used by colleges is to administer a series of tests to analyze the raw physical talents of a recruit. These tests may include the measurement of a vertical jump to test power, a 50-yard dash to observe speed, or a type of agility test to measure lateral movement. Each of these test examples are excellent indicators of raw ability for almost every sport. The measurement of power, speed and lateral movement are helpful because only small improvement can be witnessed in these areas over time, as compared to the mechanical skill–type improvement.

If you volunteer your personal time for a tryout which can lead to a scholarship payoff you should enter the session in great physical condition. Your high level of physical conditioning can only improve your chances if there is a fatigue factor built into the test. The athlete should concentrate his or her efforts in having the mechanical aspects of his or her game fine-tuned to a level of perfection. To prepare for a raw skills test, the athlete should practice commonly used drills for quickness, speed, agility, and reaction. Chances are that the college staff will be more interested in the raw skill test results than the mechanical skills because it compensates for an "off-day."

I strongly suggest that the athlete who commits to a tryout do two things immediately after making the commitment. First, try to find out what specific tests will be employed at the tryout; and second, get with your coach to plan the best training schedule to help you become fully prepared for the task at hand. One more point regarding your tryout: If you don't train hard for it, you are probably not as interested as you might think you are. And if you don't train, it will show. Hard work is the only way to achieve any worthwhile goal.

The tryout can prove to be a great opportunity for any athlete to showcase his or her abilities. Many tryout athletes like to arrange their on-campus tryout to include a campus tour and tryout in the same day. This type of scheduling is a great means to eliminate the need for a second visit. It saves money, too! If an athlete is traveling a great distance from his home for a tryout, it would be highly desirable to arrange similar tryouts and campus visits at two or three colleges in the same geographical area on successive days.

Note: The tryout can be a helping hand to satisfy your scholarship goal; however, tryouts cannot be conducted legally by every college. Before you commit to a tryout at any college campus, be sure it is legal. Member institutions with NCAA affiliation cannot conduct a tryout of any type. NAIA-affiliated colleges can. Junior colleges often utilize the tryout system, but check with the NJCAA before accepting a tryout offer.

Chapter VII
Six Types of Scholarships

As I stated earlier, this book is written for you to gain a thorough knowledge of what athletic scholarships really are all about. It is important to know the different types of scholarships that are awarded each year so you will be able to have a working vocabulary and thorough awareness of what is available to you when the opportunity presents itself. You may have assumed in your own mind that a scholarship is always a complete payment of tuition, books, fees, and more. This is not always true. As a matter of fact there are actually six different types of grants. You will see in the following pages just how each of these scholarship packages work and what you can be prepared for when a college recruiter comes knocking at your door.

Full four year grant. This is an award of room, board, tuition, and books by the institution to the athlete. This type of grant is obviously awarded only to the very, very talented. The full four year grant was a very common scholarship up until the early seventies. The full four year grant is almost a thing of the past, however, Although very lucrative, this type of grant is being discouraged by more and more conferences around the country each year. The decision to limit the four year grant coincided with the additional initial financial burdens associated with funding women athletes as described by Title IX. The additional expense in fielding virtually twice as many competitive teams caused athletic departments to attempt to stop the escalating costs of doing business. And scholarships represent one of the largest of all expenditures.

In the past if you signed a four year grant-in-aid you were signing a binding contract; therefore, the institution was responsible for your four years in school. If you become disenchanted and decided not to participate in the program anymore, or even violated rules and were dismissed from the squad, the school was still legally bound to fulfill the terms of the contract—to pay the full four years. Colleges across America have been looking for ways to reduce expenses, so to coincide with the 1975 legislation passed by the NCAA to reduce the number of athletes receiving scholarships on each athletic team, many conferences agreed to change the grant-in-aid itself. The thought behind it was to be able to drop players at the end of the year if the athlete quit or broke university regulations. The termination of that contract would allow the school to offer that scholarship to someone else and not carry an undeserving athlete for four years. If you are awarded this type of contract, you must successfully meet academic eligibility requirements each year and live up to the regulations of the school and coaching staff. The four-year award is an extinct term within NCAA member schools.

The *full one year renewable contract* has basically replaced the four year grant. This contract will be the hardest contract for you and your parents to fully understand. Legally this scholarship is awarded to a deserving athlete for a one year period of time. It will provide room, board, tuition, academic fees, and books. This scholarship is automatically renewed at the end of each school year for four years if the following conditions are met:

• The athlete successfully passes academic courses in the classroom to meet the eligibility standards of the college or university, as well as meeting entrance requirements as stated by the university and the Proposition 48 Index.

• The athlete lives up to his obligations to the coaching staff such as going to practices, attending meetings, getting medical treatment to heal an injury, etc.

• The athlete does not violate university standards of behavior (drug violations, police record, etc.).

As you read your one year contract you will not find the word "renewable." The recruiter will probably tell you that his conference or governing body (NJCAA, NAIA, or NCAA) has agreed to offer contracts for one year periods of time. He is probably being sincere in telling you that the agreement is to award this scholarship "in good faith" for the duration of your career but he is legally only allowed to offer you a one year grant. The only recourse you may have in this matter is to ask the team members of that institution if the school has been living up to its agreements of renewing past contracts. The players or players' families will be able to answer this question for you since it directly affects their personal happiness and well-being. I recommend strongly that this question regarding "good faith" be asked on the campus visitation. Also, one can simply pick up the telephone and call one or two families of the college team members in your area to ask if they are aware of any previous examples where a deserving athlete who complied academically, athletically and socially was denied an annual renewal. It is not likely that the college will be trying to deceive you, but you should check for yourself. The college's athletic program depends strongly on its reputation of fair and honest dealings. It would not take many "wrong-doings" to give the particular program a bad reputation, so the recruiter will usually tell you like it is when discussing the contract itself.

College scholarship negotiations should not always focus on simply the fees. The length of time stated in the contract may become a very important consideration when you are evaluating a college or colleges which interest you. The *one year trial grant* has a limited value in terms of duration although it could be just as attractive in terms of financial value. The trial scholarship will be a verbal agreement between you and the institution. In this case the athlete will sign a normal one year agreement, but he will be fully aware that after the first year his or her future with the sports program depends solely on a year-ending favorable review of performance, grades, attitude, or the team's need for your talent.

The one year trial is very similar to the renewable grant we discussed earlier. The only difference between this award and the one year renewable award is the verbal agreement you have with the coach recruiting you. Grants offered on a trial basis may be full or partial grants. If you are on a trial, it is obvious that your best athletic and academic performance is paramount.

The *partial scholarship* is exactly what it says it is—a grant of partial aid. The partial grant is very common in the smaller colleges and in sports programs that offer a limited number of awards in a particular sport(s). When you sign to a partial grant you may receive any part of a full scholarship or any combination of parts of a whole scholarship. You may receive books, tuition, meals, or housing. You may agree to a combination of the parts; therefore, you may receive room and board, books and tuition, tuition and housing, or the like. Thus, a partial grant is any part of the whole grant-in-aid.

Let's look at a simple example. A college allots three full scholarships for a new women's swimming program. In order to attract a larger number of talented swimmers, the coach decides to give partial scholarships. The coach then scrutinizes the talent available and signs a diver for tuition, gives room and books to a breaststroke specialist, and meals to a top freestylist. Thus, the swimming team attracts three talented performers in different areas of competition by breaking up one scholarship. The coach can then use the other two scholarships in a similar way or choose to award full grants.

The partial scholarship is probably the most flexible and negotiable type of grant awarded. Your partial grant may cover books, for example, and enjoy an outstanding first year. After this success you may approach the coach and ask to renegotiate for an increased amount of aid. Many hundreds of athletes around the country attend a college on a partial athletic grant as freshmen and develop their talents and team contributions to become full scholarship recipients by the time they graduate!

You should know that a partial scholarship does not mean that the college expects part-time loyalty and dedication from you. You will be expected to conduct yourself according to the rules spelled out by your coach and institution.

Another form of partial grant is available to out-of-state students when the college wants to attract athletes from another state or another part of the country. This form of award is called the option of *waiving out-of-state fees*. The school will therefore give an out-of-state player the opportunity to attend the college for the same amount of money charged to in-state students. This out-of-state waiver is in many cases more attractive financially than some partial grants. You will almost always find this type of option given by state-supported colleges or universities because very few (if any) private schools differentiate between in-state and out-of-state student fees.

The possibilites of a *combination scholarship* award are sometimes used. Some programs, in an attempt to attract top athletes, may waive out-of-state tuition as well as offer you a partial grant. As we have discussed earlier, your agreement to play at a college as a scholarship athlete is entirely a negotiable happening.

Another form of financial assistance used by colleges all across the country is common to every student, athlete or not. It is financial aid. Financial aid may be awarded to you by your filling out the necessary forms at the institution or institutions you are thinking about attending. Also, you can see your high school guidance officer about completing a Financial Aid Form (FAF) or a Family Financial Statement (FFS), or to see if you qualify for a Pell Grant. The FAF is administered by the College Scholarship Service (1-800-772-3537) from two mailing locations: CSS, Box 380, Berkeley CA 94701 and CSS, CN-6300, Princeton NJ 08541. The FFS is administered by the American College Testing Program (319-337-1200) from P. O. Box 1000, Iowa City, IA 52243. Before departing from this discussion of need-based loans and grants, please note that the Federal Student Aid Information Center has a toll-free number (1-800-333-4636) available to investigate guaranteed loans, federal based loans, low-interest loans, Perkins Loans, Pell Grants, etc. Should you qualify for financial aid and combine that revenue with some athletic scholarship aid, you may have a very attractive combination package of financial assistance.

We have now discussed the different types of grants-in-aid offered. We have also mentioned the different types of financial aid packages available to you through the college institution or by working through your guidance counselor. Do not confuse financial aid with the grant-in-aid. Financial aid is available to every student in the country because of hardship or low family income. A grant-in-aid is the college's way of subsidizing an athlete's education through athletic revenues or funds.

Chapter VIII

The Questionnaire:
Beginning of the
Recruiting Process

Remember, it is your senior year that you have the opportunity to show the finished product of your athletic skills. It is important that you demonstrate your specialty with excellence and determination. Many athletes are recommended to colleges each year, but the athletes that perform well are the winners in the battle for financial grants that are awarded. Before I discuss your senior year, let me give you an example of the most common pitfall of senior athletes each year. It is very important that you are aware of this pitfall so you are not left wondering "what happened?" at the conclusion of your high school career.

I think the senior athlete is caught in an unfortunate situation, since he can only compete against the competition of his league or conference in his geographical location. When you excel against the competition in your league or conference you must realize that your achievement may be excellent, but when you are being considered for a college scholarship your talents are being compared with the talents of other players or performers from many geographical locations.

Never be satisfied with your performance. Always work to improve. Just because you are the best in your area doesn't mean that you are the best in your position or your specialty from a larger geographical area. Do not just "coast" to win. Be a dominating performer against every opponent each time you compete. If you do your best and perform consistently, you will be taking a great step in achieving the goal you set: to win a college athletic scholarship.

With the college scholarship in mind, let's discuss how the recruiting process begins and many of the intricacies which are being observed by the college of the recruit. A recruited athlete is any athlete who has been personally contacted for information concerning his athletic talents. You may be contacted by a representative of a college by mail, phone or a personal contact. The personal contact may be carried out through the supervision of the coach or at your home directly with you and your parents. It is from the time of this contact until the day you sign your scholarship that you must demonstrate both efficiency and citizenship along with your skill.

College coaches and recruiters are looking for athletes who demonstrate the ability to perform at a high level of competition, as well as the ability to integrate personal mannerisms with his or her teammates. What I'm really saying is that you must show your best behavioral characterisitcs. If you show no interest or indifference to the college contacting you, you may limit your chances with that program.

Let's look at an example of the most common procedure in contacting an athlete to begin the recruiting process. Early in your senior year (sometimes late in your junior year or earlier) you may receive a form letter saying that your coach has recommended you as an athlete who has enough talent in your sport to play successfully for the college contacting you. The letter will, in most cases, include a questionnaire or standardized form asking many different questions about your personal background. In most cases it will also ask about your interest in that college. When you receive this early contact, fill out the questionnaire and return it promptly. If you are asked a question on the form such as, "Are you interested in our school?" I strongly recommend that you respond with a positive "yes" answer. Keep all avenues open until the decision-making process takes place. You may not be overly interested at the time you fill out the questionnaire, but later on in the recruiting procedure your feelings may change after you learn more about the college.

When you are filling out the questionnaire you should be very honest in answering each item of inquiry on the form provided. Remember that your abilities may be sound and acceptable for some schools, but not up to par for another college. Keep in mind that there is a proper school for you, and that the most desirable school is not always going to be the biggest school. By your honesty you may save yourself a lot of time and trouble in selecting the proper college for you. Remember the college's evaluation of your talent, behavior and academic progress will usually chronologically follow the questionnaire. The questionnaire will provide the college with pertinent information about your personal background and academic needs. The questionnaire can provide an institution the opportunity to redirect your course work toward its requirements. Maybe you need an additional math course to qualify.

Only those athletes who have previously shown film of their play or have personally had their performance observed have the clear answer that the college has okayed the athlete for a scholarship. Be sure to know your status for scholarship aid by asking the questions found in the "probing" portion of the "Five P's of Selling" section of this book. Finalize your position with each college. Ask them to make a decision about your skills as soon as possible. After the college approves you as a scholarship recipient you can begin to cultivate an interest in the benefits of attending the college which offered you the athletic scholarship aid.

Your opinions of certain colleges early in the recruiting process are subject to change. When you have the opportunity to find out more about different schools you will discover that each college has many good features. Also keep in mind that you want to pick a college situation where your athletic abilities as well as your academic background are conducive to the type of intercollegiate program you prefer. (I will discuss your selection of a college in a later chapter.) Let's look at an example of some different colleges and how each may differ in their opinions of your statistical analysis. Just as your opinions of colleges will change as you learn more about each, so will the opinions of colleges change the more each learns about you.

You are a high school fullback in football. You are 6'0" tall and weigh 190 pounds. Your football speed (which is usually measured by the 40-yard dash) is 4.8 seconds. You receive questionnaires from College A, College B and College C.

College A investigates your information and declares that the height, weight and speed meet their specific needs in their program's fullback position. The college coaching staff decides to further investigate your academic background and playing ability. After contacting your coach for film and evaluating the film as a staff, College A feels you have outstanding athletic talents, and since the college employs the same type of offensive system that your high school did, the transition from high school fullback to college fullback would be very natural.

College B is different. College B does not employ the same offense as your high school did and only play with two halfbacks—and no fullback. Your reputation is excellent so College B decides that your height, weight and speed in their system are suitable to the football program's needs at the defensive end position. This college will continue to investigate your talents and abilities, but will keep the thought in mind that your greatest contribution to their program will most probably be as a defensive end. (And let me caution all readers: don't assume you will be a fullback, or even that any program is going to change for you. Ask which position is most likely for you to play. Remember to probe!)

College C reads the same information on its questionnaire and decides that your height, weight and speed are good enough to play at some position on their team, but are not quite sure at which position you can make the greatest contribution. This college decides to look further at your athletic talents and academic background. You are considered to be an athlete who can play "somewhere." College C believes your contribution to their program may not be necessarily made at either defensive end or fullback as the other two colleges did. They are simply impressed with you as an athlete who can play some position in their football program. This decision will probably not be decided until after you attend the college as a freshman.

Colleges A, B and C are different but each one will conduct a thorough investigation and evaluate your talents by watching film, going to one of your games, or watching you practice. You may be talented enough to play at your same high school position, but maybe your best collegiate potential will be best realized at another position. So by your accurate reporting you have attracted attention and furthered your chances at three different colleges by possessing the basic athletic requirements peculiar to three entirely different football programs.

And let's go one step further. College D looks at the same information and decides that your basic height, weight and speed do not meet their football program's expectations or their particular needs at specific positions. Your honesty may eliminate College D from your selection process, but you have to be realistic in your future plans. You want to find the best football situation for your. If your basic God-given talent does not measure up to the talents of those participating at College D, you might not have been satisfied at that particular school anyway. The happy athlete is one who has a fair chance to demonstrate his skills in order to win playing time.

A similar evaluation process takes place when a college scans your questionnaire to evaluate your academic progress and potential abilities as a college student. Each college or university will have a different admissions procedure. Each college adheres to its own standards. Some colleges use your high school diploma as a means of acceptance. Some colleges place a greater emphasis on class rank, while others use ACT (American College Test) or SAT (Scholastic Aptitude Test) scores as a primary form of measurement. Still others use both grades and test scores. The most common standard method to measure academic progress is the cumulative grade point averge (GPA). When compiling a student's GPA every course taken in high school is averaged together. Most GPAs are reported on a 4.0 scale. A is the equivalent of 4.0, a B is 3.0, a C equals 2.0, and a D, 1.0. An F is recorded as 0.0. So you might be able to compute your own GPA. (Be sure to read the chapter in this book titled "Understanding Your Academic Standing.")

When you report this information on your questionnaire be sure to state the cumulative GPA and the period of time for which it was computed. For example, you might report a GPA of 2.75 over six semesters. Since each school uses a slightly different method of selecting their student athletes, your accurate reporting can help you. Work with your guidance counselor to report accurately all pertinent academic information on your questionnaire.

If you have excellent grades you will be academically attractive to every school who scrutinizes your personal data. Your good grades alone will cause many colleges with high admission standards to follow up on your progress in athletics. Good athletes are hard to find, but good athletes with excellent grades are even harder to find. If you are a good student make sure you let it be known. Good grades are as good a selling point as you may have.

Accurate reporting of a poor or average GPA can also work to your advantage. A college recruiting representative or coach may see that your GPA is not quite up to his college's entrance requirement. At another college your GPA may be slightly above the standard. In either case, above or below, your accurate reporting will alert the college interested in your talents. In each of these examples, if a college is interested in your talent it will alert you to the fact that you are a "borderline" case. In a borderline case, if you are slightly above the standard you will be told of admissions requirements and become aware of the entrance cutoff. You will then have a clear-cut idea of what kind of grades you must maintain until graduation day in order to be accepted. If you are slightly below the entrance cutoff the college's representative will alert you as to what grades you must earn by senior gradua-tion to gain admission for that particular college.

If the questionnaire asks a question, answer it. If you do not know an answer or a question doesn't apply to you, respond with "does not apply," or "do not know." If the questionnaire asks you for a SAT score, report both verbal and math portions. If you have not taken this test or plan to take it soon respond with a "plan to take SAT on such and such date." This information will alert the recruiter to the fact that you have made plans to take the test, when you will take the test, and the approximate time he can ex-pect to find out the results. It is ultimately the athlete's respon-sibility to sign up for the national tests. I strongly suggest that the earlier you do so, the better off you'll be.

If you are filling out a questionnaire in your junior year and you are asked about courses you have taken, do not be afraid to list the courses you will take in your senior year. For example:

Algebra   yes
Algebra II   yes
Geometry   yes
Calculus   to be taken senior year
Trigonometry   no

Why the questionnaire? The questionnaire form you receive is not a souvenir from a college. Your questionnaire will be used by the college as a reference form. Do not hold the questionnaire in your possession for along period of time. It shows a lack of in-terest. A long delay causes the recruiter to question your ability to be thorough in completion of a written assignment. Return it promptly, accurately and neatly. All information will likely be used for the following reasons.

It is likely that your name and address will be used to send you printed material and literature about the college. Your phone number is important so the recruiter can call you to set up home visits, to know more about your family and interests, or to contact you about visiting the campus. As has already been discussed, the information about your size, position or specialty, and speed can be used by the recruiter to quickly evaluate your potential as an athlete. If you are asked for your uniform or jersey number, indicate this number so the college evaluating your film or the observer watching you perform can quickly identify you.

Any information pertaining to your coach's name, school address or school phone number is very important since the college will need to call or write your coach for a recommendation of your talent. The coach will become a very important part of your successful attempt to win a grant since he can discuss your abilities with the college and send film or videotape of your performances. On the following page is a sample questionnaire which has been correctly filled out by a prospective softball candidate.

Note: Be sure to include a typed schedule of your games or matches along with the questionnaire. Very few forms will ask for this information. Your diligence will help the recruiter plan his schedule. By mailing your schedule the chances of the coaches watching you play increase. Should your season be already finished include the schedule of a second sport, AAU meets you plan to compete in, or summer league games. All colleges are interested in your athletic ability, and this type of schedule will help them to see you perform.

If the recruiter is aware of your schedule he may have the opportunity to watch you play on another team's film. And that team may be located 100 miles away. Coaches tend to recruit a geographical region, not just individuals. He may see that on your schedule is a game against another team with a highly touted athlete of its own. By having him come to evaluate that particular game you ensure yourself a fair chance to be evaluated. That's all you can expect. A fair chance. It also forces that same recruiter to watch you play during his very busy schedule. By watching a game or scrimmage with more than one prospect, he can budget his time more efficiently. But most importantly it can keep you in his plans. Remember, you are competing not only for a scholarship, but also for the recruiter's time. Give yourself every opportunity to be noticed. When a baseball coach goes to see another pitcher pitch, it is very hard for him *not* to watch you if he knows your name. The same would be true with an offensive lineman who plays opposite a scholarship-prospect defensive lineman

College N Softball Questionnaire

Your talents as a softball player have been recommended to us. Please fill out this form and return at your earliest convenience.

High school: __Apex High School__   Coach: ___Ms. Alice Lee___

Address: __1821 Laura Duncan Rd.__   Coach phone: (919) 362-1411

City, state, zip: __Apex, NC 27571__   School phone: (919) 362-1416

Prospect's name:__Caroline Page__   Nickname:____Cara____

Street address: 1880 Summit Drive   Parent: __Robert Page__

City, state, zip: __Apex, NC 27571__   Date of birth: __10-24-69__

Other varsity sports: ____Tennis (three years)____

Height: __5'8"__ Weight: __135 lbs.__   Best playing position: Pitcher

Bats: Right X Left__ Switch __ 2nd best playing position: __Shortstop__

Throws: Right X Left __ Softball honors? Triangle AAA 1st Team

Can you pitch? Yes Fast pitch? Yes Slow pitch? No

Class rank: 121__ in class of 265   GPA: 2.42

PSAT: Verbal 480 Math 450   SAT: Verbal 500__ Math 490

PSAT—test date: 1/22/85   ACT composite: NA

All major courses complete to date: English I, English II, English III, Algebra I, Geometry, Algebra II, Spanish I, Spanish II, U.S. History, World Geography, Biology, Adv. Biology, Chemistry, Sociology. Senior year plans to take Physics, Calculus and English Lit.

Additional Comments: Please note the attached schedule of games for my senior season. Video available from Coach Lee.

Signed: _____   Date: __9-9-85__

in football. Another simple example is a wrestler who goes head-to-head with another prospect in a state tournament. Show that recruiter you are better than "the other guy."

I strongly recommend that you type the questionnaire for legibility. If typing is not possible be sure to print so it can be read easily and without error. Be sure to proofread the information you supply to see that the form has been completed accurately. Once you've completed the form be sure to mail it at once.

The questionnaire is the first important step in a successful attempt in achieving the scholarship goal. The second step is to be sure that some form of follow-up takes place between your coach and the college(s) contacting you. You should keep an accounting of all correspondence made with each college or university. These records should be kept on file so that you have a record of every time you had contact with each school's recruiter/coach assigned to you. It may help you to decide which school has shown the most interest in you. Keep in touch with your coach to know what type of follow-up procedure has been done by each college. When you learn that a film has been sent to College A, put a sheet of paper into that school's file saying "game film vs. Seneca High School sent to College A on December 17th." Another example might include a piece of paper in your file saying "College A came to watch me practice on March 10—hit the ball well." Or "College A came to match vs. Albany—won 6–0, 6–3."

Step number three in the recruiting process is to keep an account of all information and date each piece of literature to help you know exactly when you received it. As the recruiting procedure continues you may have a great many notes and much literature in your files. This information will prove to be very helpful in your selection of the proper college. The selection process will be discussed in a later chapter. But another reminder is to the athlete who does not understand where he or she stands with any college regarding a firm scholarship offer: Ask questions just like the college asked you via questionnaire.

In summary, the recruited athlete must promptly and accurately keep account of all dealings with each interested college. First, accurately and promptly return the questionnaire to start the recruiting process. Be sure to include your schedule. Second, know what follow-up evaluation procedure has been executed by each school. Keep efficient records. Take the time to file mailings. Record and date telephone conversations and, finally, keep on file all information you receive from each college to aid in your future decision-making process.

Chapter IX
Selecting a College
and Signing a Scholarship

Selecting the Proper College for You

This book is not designed to tell you which specific college to attend. It is merely a guideline to give you a clear understanding of all the variables which must be considered when attending a college on an athletic scholarship.

An athlete has to evaluate the academic as well as athletic advantages of the college or university. With a better understanding of the points covered in this chapter the athlete will have a working knowledge about his individual needs. The academic atmosphere must be compatible with the athletic climate if the athlete is going to be a successful student-athlete.

Learn as much as you can about each school you are considering. Consult with your guidance counselor, your coach, and any students you know at the college. Fully investigate the pros and cons of each college. Ask questions of qualified people. Read as much available literature as is possible to formulate your own personal opinions. As you evaluate each phase of the athletic and academic spectrum keep in mind that you are choosing the best institution for you.

In athletic-oriented families, the parents and teenage athletes usually have a "favorite" team. If your favorite team is recruiting you, don't allow your emotions to carry you away. Evaluate each school as if you never knew it existed. By doing it in this manner you will be thorough and complete in making your decision. During my college coaching career I had the opportunity to observe my school compete against athletes who chose to go to rival institutions because it was the family's favorite. In no less than three cases the athlete never considered the academic offerings and had to select an alternate major field of study because the favorite college didn't offer a degree program for a specific area of interest.

I strongly suggest that you utilize the Select-O-Gram (see Appendix B) in order to systematically select the proper college for you. The Select-O-Gram will help you to evaluate each of the criteria you must measure. In selecting a college an athlete must look at the following general categories: (1) academic atmosphere, (2) school social life, (3) athletic facilities, (4) your health, (5) the athletic staff, (6) your individual sport, (7) the campus, and (8) administrative variables.

The Select-O-Gram will make you look for specific items, some of which you might not be aware of. Many times in my recruiting experiences parents have asked me, "What questions should I ask? I'm not familiar with athletic recruiting." Another familiar phrase is, "No one in our family has ever attended a college. Can you tell us about your school." These are honest and sincere questions. In the same respect, I have met with families who pretended to be completely informed about the recruiting process but who do not ask pertinent questions.

Before utilizing the Select-O-Gram, carefully read about each of the 60 items an athlete should consider. You will know what to look for in your reading. Your campus visitation will be more enlightening when you look for specific items. But most important you will be thorough in your selection.

Academic Atmosphere

1. *General academic reputation of the college.* Be aware of the public image the college projects. Check with the guidance counselor when considering any college, especially one of which you were not previously aware. If you go to your public library I'm quite sure you'll find a myriad of books on this subject.

2. *Your intended major.* Does the college have the *exact* course of study that you want? If not, how close is the substitute curriculum? If you are still undecided but interested in two different fields, it would be advantageous to have both options available.

3. *Can you enlarge or specialize in your intended major study area?* Example: You may want to major in business administration. Does the college offer you the chance to stay in the college of business but to select a specialized major study curriculum in accounting, banking, finance, real estate, business management, or others? Check to see if the curriculum is flexible so that you might enlarge your course work to fit your needs. An example of an enlarged curriculum might be combining a general business degree with courses in electrical engineering to pursue a business career in electronics.

4. *Number of students in average classroom* (excluding general freshman courses). How many students can you expect to have in each of your classrooms? The smaller the number, the better your chance to receive more individualized teaching.

5. *Curriculum change in your sophomore or junior year.* Is the school large enough to accommodate a change to another major in the middle of your four years? Many students enter college with one thing in mind but decide later to change their major study field. You may also investigate the college's policies on

starting with a general liberal arts curriculum with intentions of making a decision on your major course of study after a year or two at the college.

6. *Does the college allow you to arrange your schedule to avoid conflicts with athletic practice time and your classroom schedule?* Be sure to find out if the college allows special privileges to athletes in order to avoid scheduling conflicts. You need to have the opportunity to excel in both the classroom and on the playing field. You don't want to miss either a class or a practice session. One method of scheduling advantage is to have athletes pre-enroll to get early morning classes or early afternoon laboratory sessions.

7. *Proctored study hall facilities for freshman athletes.* Does the athletic department provide a special area for its athletes to study? Study hall should be proctored by a coach, graduate student or professor in order to ensure you an advisor as well as a quiet place to study. I strongly recommend a college with a strong study hall program. No matter what high school strengths you have, the study hall provides more than just a room to study. It will allow you to get into a routine. It will help to establish strong study habits. It also ensures a daily time period to study. Remember that the scholarship athlete is expected to compete against equally talented nonathletes in the classroom. And the nonathletes are not obligated to practice a sport in the afternoon.

8. *Does the athletic department provide tutoring?* Both group tutoring sessions and individual tutors provide help for the athlete in problem courses. Is the tutoring provided at the expense of the athletic department? Know what limitations are placed on the use of this privilege. Also, find out if the tutor provides transportation to the session or if the athlete must find transportation. If the athlete must drive to a tutor's house in order to receive help, the tutoring privilege can become both inconvenient and costly. Remember, to be a quality student your time is very valuable. By having the tutor come to you, your limited study time can be used to its fullest capacity.

9. *Athlete graduation ratio.* Ask about the college's graduation percentage of students who enter as freshmen. Compare this

figure with the percentage of athletes in your sport who graduate. If the athlete's figure is higher, you can conclude that the athletes are receiving proper guidance and tutoring assistance. If the percentage of athletes who graduate is lower than the student body percentage, you may question the assistance you might receive if you choose that particular program.

10. *Athletic department's attitude toward academics.* Tutoring, scheduling assistance, study halls, proctored study session, and academic counselors are visual clues to the athletic administration's attempt to help the athletes. Ask some of the athletes in the program to share some of their insights on this subject.

School Social Life

11. *Are you comfortable around other team members?* To be successful at any endeavor you should feel comfortable with the people involved. See if you feel comfortable around the players who are already in the program. Remember, the players you meet while visiting the campus will become your new teammates if you decide to attend that institution. Don't just meet the senior star players either. A little common sense will tell you that the senior athletes will be gone when you arrive on the scene.

12. *What were your impressions of the "nonathlete" students you met?* Did the students you met at the college meet you socially? These students will become your classmates, friends and fans. You can get a good impression of the self-esteem you might expect from the attitude of the nonathletes.

13. *Are there any social stigmas about being an athlete?* Did you feel that the athletes were outcasts at social functions? You might see that social interaction outside of the "athletic fraternity" may be difficult for you if this question can be answered affirmatively. Is being a "jock" an academic stigma?

14. *Any social advantages to athletes?* If your visit gives you the impression that athletes are held in high regard by students and alumni, you might expect the same. Are athletes awarded free admittance to all athletic events? Can an athlete expect the

publicity he earns in athletics to expand to student body acceptance? Community acceptance?

15. *Campus entertainment.* There are many different forms of campus entertainment. Movies, theatrical performances, art shows, concerts, fraternities, sororities, campus radio, and game rooms are examples. On-campus entertainment can be an enjoyable experience at little or no expense to the student. One of my favorite on-campus treats was watching the other athletes perform at a highly competitive level in other sports.

16. *In-town entertainment.* Cultural attractions, good restaurants, discos, etc. provide different releases from your weekly routine. If there are other colleges in town you might enjoy the entertainment provided by another institution.

Athletic Facilities

17. *The locker room.* You will spend a great deal of time here. The locker facility provides an adequate area to dress, shower and store your personal equipment. Are all pieces of practice and game equipment provided? Is the equipment reasonably new, especially the protective equipment (like helmets in football)? The locker room should demonstrate some "team pride" by the general neatness of the room itself.

18. *Training room facilities.* The training room should be equipped with up-to-date equipment that works. Is the room large enough to meet the needs of your sport? Can you rehabilitate a minor injury with the equipment available to you? Do not overlook this facility.

19. *Location of athletic facilities.* Good facilities should be planned for the convenience of the athlete in mind. Do you have to dress at Site A, drive or bus to practice at Site B, and return back to shower at Site A? Then do you need to drive to eat at Site C and sleep at Site D? Be alert to notice daily convenience or inconvenience in your future routine.

20. *Practice areas.* Is your sport given an adequate area to practice? Is there a practice area which can be used for inclement weather? Be alert for safety problems. I'd hate to be practicing

wrestling in a room without protective padding on the walls. It may also be difficult to practice the parallel bar routines in a room without a high ceiling.

21. *Game facilities.* If you play a sport with a game field that is different from the practice area, look at it. Are the seats designed to help the spectators? Is the press box up-to-date? Are the dressing facilities provided at this site? Is this the place you want your parents to come to see you play?

22. *Coaches' offices and meeting area.* You will spend a great deal of time in both facilities watching films, discussing plans and mapping strategies. Is there a meeting room which can comfortably accommodate the entire squad of the sport you play? Is visual aid equipment built into the facility?

23. *Facility emphasis in your sport and in the other sports.* Is your locker room, meeting room, practice area, etc. as well equipped as the other sports? The impression you receive regarding this point may indicate the athletic department's interest level in your individual sport.

24. *Athletic housing facilities.* Is special housing provided to athletes? Find out if you will have the opportunity to select your roommate. Is air conditioning provided during the hot months? You will spend a great deal of time in your room. Be sure that the facility provides a comfortable atmosphere to study and to sleep. My first dormitory experience was alarming. I didn't sleep the night before the first game because nonathletes in my dorm were conducting an all-night pep rally. Needless to say, an athlete needs his sleep. The athlete must also have quiet during study hours. By staying with other athletes, their study time will be as precious as yours will be. If you stay with nonathletes, "quiet time" may not coincide with your schedule.

Your Health

25. *Food.* Athletes should be provided with a special menu to accommodate their large food demands. Both the quality and the quantity of the food must be adequate for the physical demands you place on your body. Is the eating facility kept clean?

You will not be lucky enough to be eating "mom's finest" home cooking, but you will be eating at the same facility for four years. Evaluate the food.

26. *Adequate use of trainers.* Your sport should have an adequate number of qualified athletic trainers to service your team's needs. Athletes do get injured from time to time. Having a qualified person available to promptly apply treatment to any injury ensures your personal safety. Immediate treatment also helps to reduce the recovery period of most injuries.

27. *Adequate medical staff for consultation.* If an injury is serious in nature the trainer will refer you to a qualified physician. Know that the college's training staff consults an experienced team of qualified doctors who have a working knowledge of treating athletic injuries.

28. *Campus hospital or infirmary.* From time to time you may become ill and need this service. The facility must have up-to-date facilities, qualified supervision, and easy around-the-clock accessibility in order to provide useful service to the student in need.

29. *In-town hospital facilities.* A nearby hospital is an important consideration. The hospital can provide more efficient services than the campus infirmary and training room. The hospital should provide an adequate facility to diagnose injury, take X rays or perform surgery. No one wants an athlete to be injured, but if any injury should occur you want to have the best treatment possible.

30. *Insurance protection from injuries.* Will the athletic department pay for all medical expenses incurred from an athletic-related injury?

31. *Is quality protective equipment provided?* The college's athletic budget should provide any protective equipment needed by an athlete. A mask in baseball, lacrosse or hockey is a simple example of piece of protective equipment. A brace to protect an injured knee, a rebuilt shoe for an injured foot or shoulder pads for football and hockey are examples of protective equipment.

32. *Your dormitory room.* If you are a 7'0" basketballer be sure not to select a college which provides a bed only six feet long. Is a storage area provided to allow you ample storage of

your belongings? See what type of shower facilities are provided. Some dormitories only provide a community bath on every other floor.

The Athletic Staff

33. *The athletic department.* Meet as many people as possible on your campus visitation. Try to talk to the secretaries, the athletic director and the dining hall supervisor. You should leave the campus with a distinct impression of the people in the athletic department. The most desirable impression is that of an enthusiastic staff. You will spend a great deal of time with these people, so you should feel comfortable around them.

34. *Sports information director.* Every college has a person who coordinates the athletic events with the news media. Newspaper coverage, radio broadcasts, television exposure, game programs, and publicity are supervised by the sports information director. Ask what media coverage will be directed to your hometown. It is rewarding to be able to keep your parents, coaches and friends informed of your personal accomplishments as well as the accomplishments of the team.

35. *The dormitory supervisor.* Whether you stay in an athletic facility or campus facility, try to meet the dormitory supervisor to ask questions about the rules and regulations administred in the dorm. Ask if "quiet hours" are enforced to assist nighttime study hours.

Your Sport

36. *The head coach and his staff.* Remember that the person recruiting you is only a part of your sports success. You should meet the head coach (unless he is the person recruiting you) and all assistant coaches in the program. Be sure to discuss the personal coaching habits of the person to coach you. If you are an offensive lineman in football, for example, you should make it a point to sit down and talk with the head coach and the offensive

line coach. The head coach may discuss squad expectations. The line coach might discuss his drills and what you might do to prepare yourself for the future. In both cases you will learn about each coach's personality and expectations.

37. *Your sport team's tradition and won-lost record.* Rate the team's past performances. It is a very predictable measurement of that team's future expectations. Good teams generally remain good teams, no matter what level of competition the schedule offers.

38. *Position you are being recruited to play.* Pick a program where your talents can be utilized. A basketball player who specializes in dribbling skills and control-type play may not be compatible with the needs of a fast-breaking offensive team. You should be perfectly clear of the staff's feelings about your abilities. Know what position they want you to play, then formulate your opinions about your impressions of the team's style and your place in the program.

39. *Team's style of offensive or defense.* Many times your personality will provide the answer to what team style you wish to play. Defensive standouts may do better in selecting a program that puts its best players in defensive positions. Again, look at past team performances to make your evaluation. An offense-oriented player might be more excited about a high scoring team that demonstrates a great deal of creativity in its offensive. Don't tell them what you like. Ask them what they like, then make your decision.

40. *Opportunity to play early.* If you are a highly gifted performer your interest in playing early will be of great importance to you. If you enter a program where freshmen are eligible for competition you might evaluate your chances of playing your first year on campus. If the program does not allow freshman eligibility for varsity competition, your emphasis on playing early should not be as pronounced.

41. *Opportunity to play a second sport.* If you are gifted enough to play two sports you should ask about the college policy to allow its athletes to play two or more sports. Be aware that intercollegiate play is highly competitive and most players specialize in one sport. If you perform in two sports your time will

be divided, and you will not reap the benefits of "off-season" workout sessions.

42. *Media recognition.* Your hard work and ability will seek its own level of accomplishment. If you excel you want to know that your accomplishments will be recognized.

43. *Competitive and attractive scheduling.* There are three basic scheduling procedures: (1) local scheduling, (2) regional competition, or (3) a national schedule. A national schedule usually provides a very competitive atmosphere. It also increases the amount of travel expenses to and from games. Long trips can be very exciting, but they can be very tiring too! Be sure to find out the method of travel used to and from games. A two-hour plane trip will certainly be better than a 14-hour bus ride.

44. *The other athletes.* The athletes already in the program can be your best source of information. Be sure to ask the following four questions when talking with the other athletes in the program: (1) Are the athletes happy with the program? (2) Does the coaching staff give each player a fair chance to play? (3) What is the best thing about the program as it is today? (4) What is the worst thing about the program as it is today?

The athletes' answers may go a long way in helping you to make your decision and to formulate your opinions. Remember, the athletes in the program have already experienced the life that you are considering. Ask the same questions of as many athletes as you can. You will learn a great deal from the responses.

45. *Community interest and fan support.* It is always nice to have someone interested in what you are doing. Successful team play is the key to the number of fans you have and to the interest developed in the community.

The Campus

46. *Number of miles to and from home.* It is your opinion of what distance is desirable. If you want to play in a geographical region that is a successful "hotbed" for your particular event, you may have to travel a greater distance. Consider the appropriate weather problems of the region when playing an outdoor game

(baseball or softball are warm-weather sports). The only negative aspect of traveling a great distance from home is your personal transportation to and from the campus and your higher expenses of traveling a greater distance on weekends, holidays, etc.

47. *Pleasant atmosphere for higher education.* The most negative item might be a campus located in a major traffic area or directly beside a large metropolitan airport. Can you imagine trying to study with outside interferences like jets or horns disturbing your concentration?

48. *Sufficient library facilities.* Be sure to find out the reputation of on-campus research centers. An athlete will find it very difficult to travel to and from an in-town library for constant research references. Your time will prove to be a very precious commodity if you are to succeed. Be sure to learn the library's hours of operation. A library that closes at 6:00 P.M. is not very functional to an athlete who goes to class all morning and practices the greater part of the afternoon.

49. *Can you walk to all points of the campus?* Some campuses are divided, for example, into an east and a west campus. If you must take a bus or cannot make the next scheduled class, it may be difficult to avoid a class-practice conflict in scheduling.

50. *Distance from campus housing to classrooms.* The most discouraging way to begin your daily schedule is worrying how you will get to an 8:00 A.M. class if it's a long distance from your room. Dormitories should be located within a ten-minute walk to the first class. Do students utilize bicycles to alleviate on-campus transportation problems?

51. *Distance from classrooms to athletic practice facilities.* Is it convenient to get from your classes to practice? Remember that the campus at a college or university will not be like your high school campus. In high school you could leave your last-period classroom and be in the locker room within five minutes. It will become your daily responsibility to get to classes as well as practices on time.

52. *On-campus laundry facility with a place to purchase toiletries.* An athlete's schedule is very demanding; therefore, he or she must become a very good time manager. Be alert for built-

in conveniences of everyday living. Mom won't be around to wash your clothes or tend to your needs.

53. *An automobile and parking facilities.* An automobile is a personal preference. A bicycle may be a more reasonable substitute to get around some of the larger campuses. If you have a car, be sure to see if you will be provided parking privileges. If the answer is no, your car may be a greater expense (by receiving parking citations) and a greater burden than you might believe.

Administrative Considerations

54. *Will you lose your scholarship if you receive a permanent injury?* Ninety percent of the colleges in America will continue to provide the student-athlete's scholarship aid if a permanent injury problem arises. Be sure that you are not going to a college that is in the 10 percent minority.

55. *The campus and the college.* Sometimes the campus may be too large for a student. Likewise the college's enrollment may be too small to offer an appealing college experience. Are you comfortable on the campus you are visiting?

56. *Long-range building plans or long-range improvements to facilities.* Long-range projections are nice, but everyone will improve something "some day." Remember that you will be attending the college for the next four years, not the next forty years. Be a smart listener.

57. *Short-range improvements to facilities.* The best measurement is to see the newly built practice area or locker room under the building progress. Many "promises" of new facilities are made to athletes each year to make the program seem more inviting. Look at the existing facilities or those already in the construction process to draw your conclusions.

58. *High school coach's evaluation of the athletic program.* The coach may have had some interaction with the college previously. The coach should not make your decision for you, but he can offer some constructive professional guidance.

59. *Your guidance counselor's evaluation of the academic*

curriculum at the college. Use a professional person to help in your selection. Don't ask the counselor to pick the "best" school. Ask the counselor about the reputation of each school your visit. Chances are that former students have previously attended the college to offer a constructive evaluation.

60. *Parental guidance.* Last, but certainly not least. Your parents are very interested in your well-being. In my recruiting travels I have found that parents essentially "officiate" the recruiting process. Parental involvement is important. Although the final decision may be left entirely to the athlete, the parents will usually offer their most sincere advice and guidance.

After close scrutiny of the 60 most important items, you should have a better awareness of each important topic. Use the descriptions for reference if necessary. Take a copy of the Select-O-Gram with you on your campus visitation to use as a complete guideline of what to see. The next step is to evaluate each item individually. Use a point system so you can determine clearly the individual characteristics of each school. The point values should be: 3—Excellent, 2—good, 1—poor, 0—not available.

By doing the rating immediately following the visit you will record your findings at the time they are most clear in your mind. As you rate each item for each college you will find that no one institution will provide excellent ratings in every category. In the same respect no college will deserve "0" or "1" marks consistently. You make the final assessment of each particular item. By using this method your opinions will be geared to your liking and your individual tastes. You will be objectively recording your opinions of each individual item under consideration at each college you visit.

Now, to find a simple way to arrive at the all-important decision, simply add up the points awarded for each individual college. The college having the highest total of points for all 60 items is the college for you. The point system most likely eliminates emotion from an extremely difficult decision. The totals will prove to be realisitic and valid because you, the athlete, rated each item yourself.

If there is no clear-cut winner, recheck the items that are most important to you. Making your decision can be a very time-consuming task. The decision many times becomes confusing and emotionally exhausting. Do your best to let the objective facts steer you to the proper selection. Don't allow subjective emotion to overrule the decision which will have a direct impact on your future.

There is a best choice. Make it. Don't look back over your shoulder to second-guess your decision. Make your decision become the correct one. Begin to prepare yourself for your new challenge.

After you have decided on the best college for you, announce the news. The best method of announcing your selection is to have you, your parents, or your coach contact the school of your choice immediately after arriving at the all-important decision. Make the college recruiter aware of your intentions. Decide on a convenient time for signing the grant-in-aid forms.

After contacting the recruiter or head coach at the school of your choice, do the same to each of the other institutions who have been in pursuit of your talents. Thank them for their efforts and considerations. By contacting the other colleges you allow them to offer the same grant to another deserving senior.

Signing Your Grant-in-Aid

Selecting the proper college is sometimes a difficult task because all colleges have advantages and disadvantages. But selecting the college does not allow you to sit back and relax. You should know about the grant-in-aid you will sign. You must know exactly what it means.

Do not allow the signing to be a mere formality. A grant-in-aid is a binding document between you and the college presenting it to you. Grant-in-aid documents vary from one institution to another. Read each item carefully.

I would suggest that you and your parents and your coach each read the grant-in-aid papers. If any points or items are unclear, ask to have the unclear portions explained to you in detail. I have been involved in many signings on the national letter signing date which have lasted two hours or more because of this.

Be sure to check the grant-in-aid to see that (1) your name is properly spelled in the blank provided for the "recipient," (2) the name of the college is included, and (3) that the correct value (e.g. full scholarship—one year) of the grant is defined. After you check each of these items, closely scrutinize the other guidelines and provisions. Know exactly what you are signing. Your parent (or legal guardian) will be asked to cosign the grant with you. So give that party an ample amount of time to read and understand the grant, too.

Signing the grant is a very rewarding experience. It may satisfy your greatest ambition. It may give you an opportunity to earn a college education that may not have been financially possible without the scholarship. But before you begin to gaze at the stars and bask in the glory which the scholarships affords, do one more thing. Be sure to get a copy of the grant-in-aid! Remember, it is a binding contract. Keep your copy in a safe place for future reference.

Now you can jump in the air with excitement. Congratulations for a job well done!

Sometimes athletes who sign scholarships early in the recruiting season begin to receive new contacts from other colleges. This may be exciting, but it can also be very annoying to the athlete who is happy about the decision already made.

Colleges offer two basic types of grant-in-aid contracts. The first type, the institutional grant, is a simple agreement between the athlete and the college. Signing the institutional grant legally binds the college to award the grant-in-aid to the athlete.

The second type of contract is the conference grant-in-aid. The conference grant legally binds the college to award the scholarship to the athlete, too. The only basic difference is that the athlete who signs a conference grant cannot renegotiate another contract with any other school (which commonly agrees to honor the conference grant-in-aid).

Let's look at an example of both contracts. You agree to sign a partial scholarship to play field hockey for College W. Shortly after signing, College X comes to your high school to offer you a full scholarship. If you signed an institutional grant with College W, you have the legal privilege to sign another grant with College X.

Using the same example, let's look at what happens if you signed a conference grant-in-aid. College W and College X are in the same athletic conference. If each college honors the other's contract, you would not be able to sign the second grant-in-aid to College X even if the value was greater.

Here's another example of a conference grant-in-aid signing. College Y is a college who is not a member of the same athletic conference; however, College Y honors the conference contract of colleges W and X. College Y offers you a contract after you have already signed an agreement to attend College W. You cannot sign with College Y. The conference agreement binds you to your original signing in that particular conference. The improved financial arrangement is not the issue. The conference agreement is. There are many different "conference" agreements throughout the country.

Let's examine still another example. If the same athlete who signed a conference grant-in-aid with College W should be offered a scholarship from College Z (who is not a member of the same conference agreement and does not honor the same conference binder), the athlete can legally sign a second contract with College Z.

Before you sign the conference grant-in-aid know which colleges honor that agreement. Your knowledge of the member colleges honoring the contract can save you a great deal of recruiting "badgering" should the issue arise. Signing the conference agreement will also eliminate those member institutions from any further recruiting of you.

If you should sign two different conference agreements, two different institutional agreements, or a separate institutional and conference grant, you should finalize your decision as soon as possible. The final decision will relieve the added burdens from your mind. It will also allow the college whom you declined the opportunity to use scholarship elsewhere in its search for the best available talent.

Note: I strongly recommend that you evaluate and finalize

the entire scholarship picture before you sign with any college. The double signing will basically do nothing more than confuse the issue at hand. It can also be very embarrassing to you, your family, your high school, and the colleges involved. The newspapers will be certain to print something like "Athlete confused—cannot decide." Don't damage the image of respect that you earned on the athletic field by making a bad decision.

The signing is the reward. Know the type of grant-in-aid you sign. Keep a copy of the document. Have a great career!

Chapter X
A Survey of Former Athletes

The athlete with many choices in selecting one college from a group of colleges will experience difficulty in weighing all the factors to arrive at a best choice. The difficulty comes because there are many strong points associated with the different institutions. To help you arrive at your all-important decision, I have conducted a survey with a group of former athletes in order to share some of their thoughts and perspectives regarding their decision-making process of picking a college. The subjects each attended college institutions and played one or more varsity sports while attending. I asked seven basic questions (see Appendix C):

1. The sport(s) each played
2. The college which the athlete attended
3. The college's affiliation (NCAA–men, NCAA–women, NAIA, NJCAA)

4. The number of scholarships offered to the athlete
5. The number of miles from hometown to college
6. The reasons the athlete chose his/her college
7. The reasons the athlete would choose if he/she had to go to school again

Conducting the survey was very interesting and very enlightening. I found that each athlete had a slightly different perspective about his/her choice. It was fun being an impartial bystander and having the opportunity to learn more about what people who had similar athletic goals felt about subjects which were hardly ever discussed.

In an attempt to find opinions which reflected a nationwide and broad-based feeling, I mailed over 300 survey forms. The results include all responses from 133 former athletes. These athletes came from all walks of life. Business executives, college and high school coaches, members of the clergy, school administrators, pro athletes, teachers, and graduate students were all involved in the survey. The profession with the greatest response was the coaching profession, with approximately half of the respondents being coaches (of various sports).

The 133 responses came from athletes who attended 97 colleges in 29 different states. The number of athletes, colleges and states represents a random cross sample of athletes from throughout the country. Let's look at the results of the survey to help you understand how complete and extensive a study in human opinion this really was. We will analyze each of the seven questions in greater depth to help you further analyze the results.

1. *The sports played by the athletes.* Athletes who responded to the survey participated in 14 different sports. The sports were football, basketball, cross-country, baseball, track, softball, gymnastics, golf, tennis, swimming, wrestling, volleyball, lacrosse, and rugby. The sport with the largest number of responses was football. Baseball players represented the second largest sampling in the survey.

Sixty-eight percent of the athletes played one sport; 32 percent played more than one sport. The combination of football and baseball was easily the most common combination of the two-sport athletes. The two-sport athlete was more common in the smaller colleges than the larger colleges. Each of the female athletes surveyed played more than one sport.

2. *The colleges attended by the athletes.* In order to substantiate all of the information received, I felt like it would be necessary to sample athletes from many schools. As I stated earlier, 97 different colleges were represented. The largest response came from athletes who graduated from North Carolina State University (12). The second largest participation was from athletes who graduated from the University of South Carolina (9). Eighty-five of the colleges mentioned were represented by either one or two responses each. Since colleges from 29 states were sampled, the survey tends to represent a national opinion. The surveys were intended to reach out to former athletes rather than particular schools, so small colleges as well as large universities had an equal opportunity for representation in this survey.

Hoping to achieve a random response, the survey was offered to both men and women. It is my opinion that each of the population breakdowns (men to women, etc.) are not important to serve the purpose of presenting former athletes' opinions.

One other point of interest is that virtually all of the athletes surveyed were college graduates maintaining good professional jobs. This fact is important since it eliminates negative emotion, bitterness, and regrets from the results. Negative emotion is generated by failure. By sampling only graduates the survey only questions those who have participated in programs from the freshman level through the varsity level. A greater range of experiences can be expected from the group. Having virtually all participants who are graduates also serves my reading audience well. I would like this book to be a positive influence on your future so that you can wind up, like the graduates, gainfully employed for your entire working life.

3. *The college's affiliation.* Of all athletes surveyed, 64 percent attended colleges sponsored by the NCAA. The group was also represented by 30 percent of the colleges involved in NAIA competition. The NCAA-women had only a 9 percent involvement in the survey; however, the number of graduating women

athletes is growing rapidly. Junior college participants accounted for 8 percent of the participation in the survey.

4. *The number of scholarships offered to each athlete participating in the survey.* Each athlete was asked to indicate the number of scholarship offers he or she received before selecting a college. The responses did not indicate the value of those grants offered, so some were full grants and some were partial. The two-sport athletes were not asked to declare what portion of the scholarship was paid by which of the two sports. It would be my guess that football paid the majority of those two-sport athletes' scholarship bills.

Seventy-three percent of the athletes indicated that they were offered one or more scholarships to play sports in college. Twenty-seven percent indicated that they attended the college of their choice to participate in sports without a grant-in-aid. Many of these athletes earned a grant-in-aid at a later date. Some athletes attended colleges which did not offer grants-in-aid to athletes, choosing to play without aid.

As previously stated, 27 percent of the athletes surveyed attended colleges without an athletic scholarship in the freshman year. This high percentage substantiates the fact that the walk-on athlete plays a prominent role in college athletics today. If you cannot win an athletic grant from your high school performances, do not give up on your ambition of winning a grant. Many colleges will welcome an athlete who wants to try.

Of the 73 percent offered grants-in-aid, 30.5 percent were offered one to three athletic scholarships, 12 percent were offered four to six athletic scholarships and 30.5 percent were offered seven or more grants. Many scholarship athletes indicated that the college each matriculated into was the only school to offer a full grant-in-aid. This was true in the one to three scholarship category as well as the seven or more category. In other words, these athletes had one full scholarship and all others were partial scholarships. With this information in mind, it is reasonably safe to conclude that the athlete who is highly publicized as a scholarship winner is not always one who has 100 or more scholarship offers. Media publicity and word of mouth have a funny way of distorting the everyday realisms. Keep the aforementioned facts in perspective. Fifty-five percent of the athletes surveyed had three or less grant-in-aid offers. The same 57 percent were the ones who played and graduated in colleges all around the country.

5. *The number of miles from the athlete's hometown to his/her college.* The survey indicated many different answers on how many miles athletes travel to college. Forty-six athletes indicated that the distance to college was 100 miles or less. The shortest distance was recorded by a football and rugby athlete who traveled one mile to attend San Diego State University. A University of Toledo athlete only traveled two miles. Staying close to home was most certainly a consideration of each of these athletes.

Of those who traveled greater distances to participate as athletes, 31 athletes indicated that they traveled 200 miles or more to attend college. The largest single statistic was registered by an athlete who participated in the football and wrestling program at the University of Hawaii. This athlete traveled 2,500 miles from home! The second greatest distance was indicated by a football and baseball player who attended Adams State College in Colorado. This athlete traveled 1,100 miles. A combined figure of 22,265 miles was recorded by the athletes who indicated the distance from college to home. The average distance was 237 miles. I feel that the 237-mile average indicates that all athletes in pursuit of a grant-in-aid should be open-minded about travel distances. The closest college or university to your home may or may not be the one to offer you a grant-in-aid. Since 237 miles represents an average distance, you might begin to investigate colleges in a geographical radius which is similar to the average number of miles from your hometown. After you have exhausted all leads in this radius, then broaden your investigation by pursuing leads outside the average radius.

6. *The reasons athletes chose their college during their senior year of high school.* After surveying all athletes, I found that many had a slightly different priority of the most important considerations in selecting the college they ultimately attended. Although many responses were similar, no two were exactly the same. I found that even in the cases of athletes attending the same college, each expressed different reasons for his or her choice.

I asked each subject to state the ten most important considerations in his/her selection procedure. Each subject was asked to put the reasons in order of preference. By listing the reasons in order, I was able to put a greater value on the answers at the top of the list, and a decreasing value on the lesser considerations.

By using the decreasing scale technique I was able to designate a 10-point value for the most important reason, a 9-point value for the second most important reason, 8 points for the third reason, 7 points for the fourth, and so on. The tenth consideration, therefore, received a 1-point value. If an athlete listed only three reasons for attending his/her college, I awarded 10 points for the first reason, 9 points for the second reason, 8 points for the third reason. No other points were awarded since no other responses were registered.

Let's look at the results from the survey. Remember that these responses indicate the feelings of the athlete as he selected his college during the senior year of high school. Later on in this chapter we will look at the same athletes' opinions of what to look for after each experienced his or her career.

By using the 10, 9, 8, etc. decreasing point scale, I discovered the following results. The results are given in order of the survey participants' composite preference. The first was the most popular response, the twentieth being the least popular response.

1. geographical location
2. impression from campus visitation
3. academic curriculum offered
4. head coach of school recruiting you
5. recommendation of high school coach
6. athletic tradition of the school
7. school's athletic facilities
8. opportunity to play early
9. recommendation of a friend
10. parental influence
11. recruiter of the school recruiting you
12. recommendation of alumni
13. recommendation of a former teammate

14. school's schedule of games
15. team's won/lost record
16. rapport with coaching staff of school
17. other comments (listed)
18. opportunity to play a certain position
19. graduation ratio of athletes
20. style of athletic teams—offense or defense

7. If an athlete had to pick a college again, the reasons he would use in the selection process. The same athletes were used in this survey. The results indicate that through each athlete's experiences, the selection procedure might be somewhat different. I used the same decreasing point values to arrive at the results. Let's look at the most important considerations in the eyes of experienced athletes who played sports in college. Here are the graduates' responses to what considerations should be taken into account when selecting a college.

1. academic curriculum offered
2. athletic tradition of the school
3. geographical location
4. graduation ratio of athletes
5. impression from campus visitation
6. opportunity to play early
7. school's athletic facilities
8. head coach of school recruiting you
9. rapport with coaching staff of school
10. team's won/lost record
11. promise of employment after graduation
12. school's schedule of games
13. parental influence
14. recommendation of high school coach
15. style of athletic teams—offense or defense
16. opportunity to play a certain position
17. media recognition and exposure
18. recruiter of the school recruiting you
19. opportunity to play a second sport
20. recommendation of a former teammate

I feel it is important to evaluate each consideration, but let me call to your attention a comparison. Although the same subjects were used in the survey, the results of the "before college" reasons were different than the "after college" reasons. Let's analyze the comparisons.

Geographical location is obviously felt to be a very important consideration. Athletes indicated, however, that the reasons for their personal selection of geographical location were varied. Some wanted to stay close to home. Others chose to explore a new geographic atmosphere. Some went to college in the vicinity of family relatives. Others who participated in outdoor sports traveled greater distances to benefit from the advantages of better year-round climate.

Each reader should notice the response regarding "academic curriculum offered" showed a marked increase from the "before" survey when compared to the "after" survey. Although the academic curriculum rated high in both sets of results, the college graduates made this response a clear-cut first place in the "after college" test. One could interpret this change as a need for academic fllexibility as the participant changed interest areas, or the lack of flexibility in their college's curriculum. In either case, the need to have the ability to change major study areas appears to be very important. This comparison indicates simply that the academic values and rewards far outweigh the athletic values and rewards when discussing what becomes important to the student-athlete.

Let's continue our discussion concerning academic values. The athletes surveyed placed little interest in the graduation ratio of athletes in the "before" test rating (19th); however, after reconsideration this same response rated 4th! This dramatic turnabout verifies the overall importance of academic satisfaction. This comparison leads one to believe that athletic participation is a worthwhile experience only if it leads to an academic degree!

The response "athletic tradition of the school" improved from the "before" test to the "after" test. Most athletes indicated that the basic feeling was on-the-field and off-the-field recognition as well as postgraduation benefits were greater at the more prestigious institutions.

To continue the comparison and analysis of the survey, I found that the head coach of the sport played and the opportunity to play early rated high in both "before" and "after" surveys. Athletic facilities proved to be another highly important consideration in both tests. The consistency of each of these responses indicates the overall importance of each consideration. It also indicates the need to investigate each one in great depth. We have discussed these and many more important areas in the chapter "Selecting a College and Signing a Scholarship."

People will have a great influence on your decision. The "before" survey indicates that the high school coach, the college head coach, parents, friends, former teammates, and college alumni greatly influenced athletes' decisions of which college to attend. The only three people influences who rated highly in the "after" test were the college head coach, the parents, and the high school coach. The impressions made by the college recruiter and former teammates were the only other personal opinions that were somewhat highly regarded. Personal friends' influences completely dropped from the "after" college listing.

Two responses not mentioned in the "before" test made the top twenty listing in the "after" test: "a promise of employment after graduation" and "opportunity to play a second sport." The employment outlook indicates that athletes should anticipate long-range problems associated with the academic curriculum of their choice. Geographical and local job availability could also factor into the employment outlook. The reputation of the institution many times has a great deal of effect on successfully finding employment after college. Indicating a desire to play a second sport shows that those who had the opportunity were happy about the chance. The results also indicate that those athletes who did not have the second sport opportunity wish that they had chosen a college that offered them the chance to play a second sport. If you are highly skilled in two areas, this consideration may be an important one. It was to me.

Study the results of the "before" college survey and compare the results to the "after" college opinions. Let this evidence serve as an objective aid in helping you decide exactly what items are important to you. I do feel that the results of the "after" college test indicate a more accurate result because "hindsight is 20/20." Each athlete had the opportunity to experience both the positive and negative aspects of college life. Use their experiences to your advantage. Remember that no matter what influences you to select a college it is your decision. You must attend classes; you must live there; you must travel to and from home; you must compete for a position on the team; and you must wear the reputation associated with your degree. Make the decision that is best for you.

Chapter XI
Meeting Proposition 48
Guidelines

In January 1983, the member institutions of the NCAA Division I level passed legislation for probably the most talked about recruiting rule in the last two decades. It is commonly known as "Proposition 48" or the "2.000 Rule." It has stirred quite a controversy, but rules are rules—so let's follow it closely so you can understand all of its basic requirements. Although this chapter deals specifically with this issue, it is important that an overall academic overview be reviewed in the next chapter on academic standing of the student/athlete.

Proposition 48 and the 2.000 Rule are really only affectionate names assigned to amend the NCAA Bylaw (5-1-[j]), which must be met by the student-athlete in order to participate in intercollegiate athletics and to receive athletically related financial aid as a freshman. The official language as stated in the NCAA rule:

A qualifier as used herein is defined as one who is a high school graduate and at the time of graduation from high school presented an accumulative minimum grade point average of 2.000 (based on a maximum 4.000) in a core curriculum of at least 11 academic courses including at least three years in English, two years in mathematics, two years in social science and two years in natural or physical science (including at least one laboratory class, if offered by the high school) as certified on the high school transcript or by official correspondence, as well as a (minimum) 700 combined score on the SAT verbal and math sections or a (minimum) 15 composite score on the ACT."

This rule goes into effect completely on August 1, 1988. At that time a minimum 2.00 and 700 SAT or 15 ACT will be the requirement. Until 1988, the following standards are acceptable:

Beginning August 1, 1986

GPA	SAT	ACT	For clarification:
2.2+	660	13	A = 4.000
2.1–2.199	680	14	B = 3.000
2.0–2.099	700	15	C = 2.000
1.9–1.999	720	16	D = 1.000
1.8–1.899	740	17	F = 0 quality points

To fully interpret the preceding chart we can use the first example of the student with a grade point average of 2.2 or better. This student must meet the minimum test score of 660 on the SAT or 13 on the ACT. Even if you carry a solid "B" average the 660 or 13 score must be achieved. In reverse, let's look at the athlete who scores well on the SAT or ACT—he must achieve a minimum GPA of 1.800 in core curriculum courses. Even if an athlete had 1000 SAT score, the minimum GPA must be achieved.

Beginning August 1, 1987

GPA	SAT	ACT
2.1+	680	14
2.0–2.099	700	15
1.9–1.999	720	16

These requirements demonstrate that the minimum test score will be 680 or 14, while the minimum acceptable GPA is 1.9.

Beginning August 1, 1988

GPA	*SAT*	*ACT*
2.0+	700	15

At this point, the rule will be clear as to the minimum acceptable levels of "core course" achievement in the classroom.

It may be extremely beneficial to the reader to explain that a core course is defined as a recognized academic course which offers fundamental instruction in the course area. It is *neither* a vocational or personal services course *nor* any remedial, special education or compensatory level course regardless of subject matter.

Let's discuss the specific core course areas as stated by the NCAA:

English—core courses in English shall contain instructional elements in the following areas: grammar, vocabulary development, composition, literature, analytical reading or oral communication.

Mathematics—core courses in mathematics must be designed to develop a student's basic ability to formulate and solve mathematical problems in courses such as mathematics, geometry, alegebra, trigonometry, statistics or calculus.

Social Science—core courses in social courses in natural or physical science shall include biology, chemistry, physics, environmental science, botany or geology. In addition, students must complete at least one laboratory class, if offered by the high school.

Additional Core Courses—the two remaining years of additional academic credit must be from courses attempted in English, mathematics, social science, natural or physical science, foreign language, computer science, speech, religion or philosophy.

1. Where can I get additional legal information regarding Proposition 48?

Please write to NCAA Legislative Services, P. O. Box 1906, Mission, Kansas 66201.

2. In my four years of high school I will take 16 "core" courses. Do I factor my core GPA by dividing the total number of quality points by 16 to calculate my GPA?

The NCAA encourages the student athlete to take as many

academic courses as possible. With this in mind the student can factor his or her best 11 grades from courses which meet the distribution requirements of the core curriculum.

3. Are there any exceptions to this "2.000 rule" interpretation?

No. But remember this rule only applies to NCAA Division I and NCAA Division II schools only. The NCAA Division III level as well as NAIA and NJCAA college participants will not adhere to the "2.000" guidelines. These institutions will set their own requirements, with some being more difficult and others being less stringent.

4. The distribution guidelines specify only 9 courses, not 11. What are the remaining two courses which need to be taken to meet the requirements of this Bylaw?

The additional courses can be any other *academic* courses from the four major subject areas of English, math, science or social science as well as from *academic* courses in foreign language, computer science, speech, religion or philosophy.

5. Who determines whether my courses are academic or nonacademic, thus qualifying for the core course requirement?

The decision will be made by the principal from the high school from which the student graduated.

6. Is there a formula to factor by GPA?

Yes. Grade point average is equal to the sum total of quality points, times the number of course credits, divided by the total credits completed.

7. I made a B+ in geometry. Can I use a different factor to take advantage of the plus?

No. Pluses and minuses do not receive greater or lesser quality points. The only special consideration given is to advanced-level placement courses.

Note: An exempted student must have maintained a 3.500 for his or her last four semesters of completed high school work in addition to maintaining a top 20 percent ranking in his or her high school class. The only requirement which can be waived is the "graduation from high school." Proceed with caution and only with the support of parents, guidance counselors and your principal.

Chapter XII

Understanding Your Academic Standing

Before discussing academics, I will discuss two thoughts which have already been formulated:

- A college athletic scholarship is a form of payment for fees, room and board, tuition, books, etc.
- A scholarship may be your ultimate goal, but you should have some short-term skill goals as well as intermediate and long-range goals.

There is a great deal of grandeur associated with being a student-athlete on full scholarship who achieves the goals he or she sets for himself or herself. It all sounds great! But whether you believe it or not, this book is really concerned with athletics as a means to an end. The means is your athletic ability and the end is a college education. That's right! This book was written to guide you in channeling your abilities to help you earn your way through college. Keep that point in mind as you read the key points I will make in this chapter.

One of the key coaching principles which I learned early in my coaching career was K.I.S.S.—Keep it simple, stupid. What K.I.S.S. means is that when you are planning an important game strategy or teaching a player something very important, make sure that the athlete can understand all aspects of the plan. It is with simplicity in mind that I will discuss the most important academic topics, since this chapter actually should get equal time with athletics.

Since the best way to keep a concept simple is to state the concept and explain it, I will follow just such a format by asking ten important questions and then answering each.

1. Do grades really matter?

If there are two athletes of equal athletic ability vying for one scholarship, the scholarship will go to the better student 95 percent of the time. The better student not only enhances the potential graduation ratio of each coach, but the better student is less of a risk since he will more than likely be in college for his senior year. And coaches win with seniors.

2. Does getting a scholarship mean that you are going to graduate because the athletic department will get you tutoring help, have study halls, and offer academic guidance?

Absolutely not! My freshman class of 56 scholarship athletes (the rules have changed!) saw only seven players graduate after five years. I was lucky to be one of the seven. The players who graduate are those who place academics on an equal footing with athletics and work just as hard to succeed in the classroom as they do on the playing field. Accepting the responsibility of a student-athlete is a very large undertaking.

One of my professors told me that the major college athlete who wants to be successful in the classroom as well as on the field is really at a severe disadvantage because he has to compete for a playing position with the best athletes from around the country as well as compete for a degree with the best students from around the state, but he has only 50 percent of his time to compete with other athletes or other students who devote 100 percent of their time to be successful at just one priority.

The college recruiter can tell you all he'll do for you to become a better student, but you must want to do it yourself if you will earn a degree.

3. Do athletes need to take the SAT or ACT National Tests for admission to college?

Each college or university has different entrance requirements, but most require that the student take at least either the Scholastic Aptitute Test (SAT) or the American College Test (ACT). Only a few will ask for both test results. Any athlete who is serious about college should plan to take at least one of these two national tests *prior to* the beginning of the athlete's senior season.

I think it is appropriate to mention to each reader that during a typical school year, there are only five ACT dates and only eight SAT dates. The ACTs and SATs are not the type of tests which allow for walk-in registration. There is about one month's postmark deadline prior to each scheduled test. Late registration carries an additional fee but still requires an approximate two-week postmark deadline. The results of these tests are not made available to the student until 4–8 weeks after the actual testing date. Plan accordingly.

4. How can I register for the SATs or ACTs?

I suggest that you call or write the appropriate organizations for a test registration packet as well as for sample test questions to familiarize yourself with the type of test you will be taking. The testing fee will be noted in the packet.

ACT Registration Department
P.O. Box 414
Iowa City, IA 52243
(319) 337-1270

SAT Educational Testing Service
Room J-240
Trenton, NJ 08618
(609) 771-7600

Of course, you can also visit your school's guidance office to learn the specifics regarding each test.

5. How can I compute my grade point average?

I'll give you a method, but *be sure to confirm your findings with your high school's guidance office.* Ninety percent of the high schools compute the same way, but I'd hate for you to fall short with my formula because you factored in minor course grades with major course grades.

To factor your grade point average (GPA) simply divide the total number of quality points earned in major courses by the number of major courses taken. Quality points are assigned to each final grade you earn. Any final grade of "A" earns four quality points, any "B" grade earns three quality points, and "C" earns two quality points, and any "D" earns one quality point. An "F" earns zero. Minuses and pluses do not count for or against the student.

If a student earned one "A," one "B," one "C," one "D," and one "F," his GPA would be 2.0. Simply add quality points 4 (for the "A") plus 3 (for the "B") plus 2 (for the "C") plus 1 (for the "D") plus 0 (for the "F") for a total of 10 quality points. Simply divide the total number of courses taken, 5 (because the F counts), into the total number of quality points, 10. The answer is 2.0 GPA.

• Bobby Jones earned three "A's," one "B," and six "C's" in his first two years of high school. What is his GPA? Bobby has a 2.7 GPA $(12 + 3 + 12 \div 10 = 2.7)$.

• Andrew James earned three-year totals of two "A" grades, three "B" grades, seven "C" grades, two "D" grades, and one F. Andrew has a 2.2 GPA $(8 + 9 + 14 + 2 + 0 \div 15 = 2.2)$.

• Jon David earned three B's and two C's during his freshman year. His GPA is 2.6 $(9 + 4 \div 5 = 2.6)$.

6. Can I use just my senior year's grades to figure my GPA?

Remember, you must have short-term, intermediate and long-term goals. Grades must be included in all three goals. To answer question 6 the answer is "No." To correctly arrive at your composite GPA you must use either the first six consecutive semesters' results, the first seven consecutive semesters' results, or the first eight consecutive semesters' results. Even in cases which find the ninth grade in the junior high, the ninth grade marks must be included.

7. What can I do to overcome two bad years of high school grades?

If you dug the hole, you'll simply need to do everything in your power to create better study habits and create stronger priorities toward using your time more wisely. Your short-term goal might be to complete every homework assignment and study for each test. It is amazing what one can achieve with just short-term goals.

I once had an athlete who was ranked 147 out of 148 (that's as close to the bottom as you can get!) after 2⅓ years of high school. Our staff recognized his potential during his junior football season, discussed the hole which the athlete had dug for himself, and challenged him to fill up the hole with a lot of hard work. Today, that young man is the proud owner of a bachelor of arts degree as well as a master of arts degree from two different colleges.

It's all up to you! Rearrange your priorities to include academic success along with athletic success and set some short-term, intermediate, and long-range goals. And just as you should take the time to learn the rules of your sport so you don't fall short in the fourth quarter, take the time to know where you stand academically and what grades and test marks you need.

8. Why should I worry about grades? I'm going to be a professional athlete who makes a lot of money after college.

As good as you think you are, only one in every 30 football athletes at the major college level ever get a chance to try out for a professional team. Probably only one in 20 of those makes it for a period of one to five years.

In a discussion with NCAA national champion baseball coach Ron Frasier of the University of Miami, I learned that in 19 years of ultrasuccessful recruiting of "blue-chip" athletes, only eight players succeeded to the major league level for more than a month. And that program has about 90 percent of its players sign professional contracts after college. Don't be fooled by the 90 percent figure, either, because a program like Miami's only takes the "best of the best" type baseball athletes. You may play great, but there are great players in other parts of the country. These are very startling statistics for male athletes to accept. Young women, your chances for professional athletic careers virtually do not exist at the time of this writing.

I'd like to finish answering this question with a question. Even if you do make it to the professional level of competition and play to the ripe old age of 35, what are you going to do for the next 35 years?

9. What value do you place on the academic portion of the athletic scholarship?

I always told my prospects and players that the one thing that separates a graduate from a nongraduate is that the graduate will have a choice in what he does for the rest of his life. The degree opens many doors, but the greatest part is that the doors which open will be in the graduate's interest area.

10. With the K.I.S.S. concept in mind, what is the simplest advice you can give me to achieve academic success?

Study and complete all assignments with the same pride you have demonstrated in playing your sports specialty.

Chapter XIII
Three Ways to Earn a Scholarship After High School Graduation

Former major league baseball player-manager Yogi Berra has been widely publicized for his quote "It [the game] ain't over 'til it's over." Even though he wasn't making reference to a high school student's quest for a college athletic scholarship, the quote is very appropriate in discussing the contents of this chapter.

In this book persistence has been discussed as one of the "5 P's of Selling." You and your coaches have been encouraged to keep following up on leads during different prime recruiting periods. You have learned about reasons which prove that it is never too late to start studying. The senior year has been shown to be the athlete's chance "to showcase the finished product."

Actually there are three avenues available to athletes after the senior year. That's right, three ways to continue to achieve your ultimate goal. The three methods are (1) to become a walk-on athlete at a four year school immediately following high school, or (2) to take a one year term at a preparatory school, or (3) to enroll in a two year accredited junior college who participates in the athlete's specialty. The reasons people choose the walk-on, prep, or JC route are as varied as the individuals themselves. Some athletes are young seniors and anticipate growing more during the next year or two, while others have floundered academically and seek improvement. Still others want to attend a local school to make the adjustment to college a little easier, and others desire the curriculum which is best for the student-athlete involved. Still others follow the geographical tendencies of northern players who seek prep schools, East Coast players who choose the walk-on status, and midwestern and West Coast players electing to utilize the junior college route. Each reader must make up his or her own mind as to which method is best for him or her since each has been proven to be effective. I will attempt to highlight the advantages and disadvantages of each as I see them. But again, you should make up your own mind as to which method is best for you.

The Walk-On

You may choose to become a "walk-on" athlete. A "walk-on" athlete is any athlete who participates in a four year college athletic program without the benefit of a grant-in-aid when he matriculates. Being a walk-on or nonscholarship athlete affords many advanatages. The walk-on should select a college program that offers a large number of scholarships. Also, select a program that shows a sincere interest in giving you a fair opportunity to demonstrate your abilities. I have had the good fortune of seeing many, many athletes earn grants immediately. I have also seen walk-on athletes earn a scholarship after two or three years of participation. The greatest advantage a walk-on enjoys is timing. The walk-on will be involved in the program as scholarship aid becomes available. In an earlier chapter we talked about timing being of paramount importance. The walk-on can participate in the program of his choice to improve his skills with the help of very well-qualified coaches. He can become familiar with the coaching terminology and philosophy. He can also demonstrate a high level of personal pride and character—two factors that every coach in America learns to love in athletes.

As the walk-on improves his skills, learns the philosophy, and demonstrates high moral fiber, he becomes a more worthy candidate to be a recipient of a grant-in-aid. I have known a number of walk-on athletes who earned athletic grants solely to help in the practice routine. In large athletic organizations there is a tremendous need for fielding a large squad in order to provide excellent practice individualization. One of my old walk-on football athletes, Max Runager of the San Francisco 49ers, has a Super Bowl ring today. That shows you how much we coaches know.

The best advice any walk-on can receive is simple: stick with the program. Players quit and players leave. New scholarship money becomes available each year. The old adage of "being in the right place at the right time" is the motto of industrious walk-ons.

If you understand the system employed by the coaches and you demonstrate adequate athletic skills, your chances improve greatly to earn a grant-in-aid. Any coach would rather offer a grant to an athlete whose skills he is familiar with. This is especially true if you have a specialty like the football skills of long snapping, punting, and placekicking. Some similar talents might be an unnoticed defensive specialist in basketball or a base stealer/pinch runner in baseball.

Academically the walk-on can attend the college of his choice and study the curriculum of his liking. All academic course work leads to a degree at the chosen institution. The academic advantages are strong. To be complete in our discussion of nonscholarship athletes I should point out the negative side of the ledger.

In becoming a walk-on athlete you may sacrifice a great deal of your time for little financial reward. There are no guarantees that you will win the grant-in-aid you want. You must participate in all practice and meeting sessions. You will be playing with teammates who are scholarship athletes. This sometimes is a difficult pill for the nonscholarship athlete to swallow. You will do the same amount of work and preparation as the scholarship athlete and possibly receive nothing in return. Only the confident athlete should pursue a walk-on status.

Being a walk-on will certainly be a challenge to you. You will work hard for no guarantees. You must endure the rigors of the playing field and the classroom. All this seems bad, but the walk-on is a special person who reaps many intangible benefits along the way. Being associated with the organization of players and coaches can be rewarding. You will receive quality coaching to improve your skill level to its greatest potential. You will always be involved in the program when new grants become available.

If you believe in your potential and do not want to end your playing career after being denied any scholarship assistance after high school, be a walk-on athlete. Your experiences will be worthwhile and your chances for receiving a grant-in-aid will increase with each day. Many walk-ons have succeeded in the past and many more will in the future. Just remember to "stick with the program."

The Preparatory School

The preparatory school philosophy will vary from one school to another. Generally speaking, the preparatory school is a high school who offers its student a chance to attend a fifth year of high school to complete high school deficiencies or increase skills which lead to acceptance to a four year college. Preparatory schools are attended by good students who aspire to build on requirements which can lead to acceptance to a better four year school or are attended by poor students seeking to improve the GPA to qualify for acceptance to any four year institution.

Some preparatory schools feature strong curricula in the sciences, or feature military-type discipline or feature a campus away from the social distractions which may have caused less than excellent academic performances in high school.

From a sports-offering perspective these institutions participate in a limited number of sports. The schedule is usually against similar preparatory schools, or area college freshman squads and junior varsity squads, or area junior colleges. One key plus to the student attending the preparatory school is to gain collegiate-type playing experience. And the colleges almost always recruit the best preparatory school players whom they have competed against.

Most professional people will tell you the preparatory school offers an additional year for a young person to mature, accept added responsibility, and to grow physically. One other plus is that it creates an away-from-home year for adjustment.

For the student who needs to improve his grades, the preparatory school is an excellent alternative. Most athletes who attend preparatory schools to participate in sports have already been recruited by a four year institution but failed to gain academic acceptance. They will more than likely matriculate at that college upon successful completion of the preparatory school year.

The athlete with good enough grades to attend a four year institution of his or her choice who chooses to attend a preparatory school to gain attention to athletic skills is taking a large, expensive risk. It is true that you may grow, gain speed, or get better playing opposite college-type competition; however, you are also one injury away from wasting a year of your life. Remember that the academic course work is high school course work and offers no carry-over college transfer credits.

The best utilization of the preparatory school is found by those athletes already recruited who have a place to go after successful completion of the course work. Preparatory schools are essentially advantageous for qualification to a four year institution's academic requirements.

The Junior College

Although the greatest portion of this publication deals directly with student participation at member institutions in the NCAA and NAIA, another level of collegiate opportunity exists. Two year institutions, referred to as community or junior colleges, many times offer grants-in-aid similar to the four year institution. Each junior college is affiliated with the National Junior College Athletic Association (NJCAA), headquartered in Colorado Springs, Colorado. Each member institution attempts to compete on an equal basis with member NJCAA institutions in its sport and geographical area. Active participation includes both men's and women's programs. The advantage afforded any athlete who chooses to participate in the junior college level is that he or she gets the opportunity to compete, work toward a four year degree while securing a two year degree, prepare his or her play for four year competition by participating at a better level of competition than high school, and still have the opportunity to be re-recruited as a transfer student at a four year institution.

During the 1983–84 scholastic year 460 member institutions participated in women's NJCAA competition. During that year 398 junior colleges had women's basketball programs, while only 36 competed with women's bowling teams. By taking a further look at member NJCAA institutions, you'll learn that 94 cross-country programs, 16 field hockey teams, 26 golf teams, 5 gymnastic teams, 13 skiing teams, 29 soccer teams, 207 fast pitch softball and 50 slow pitch teams, 25 swimming and diving entries, 197 tennis programs, 89 outdoor and 48 indoor track programs, and 257 volleyball entries existed. During the same school year, 529 member NJCAA colleges participated in men's sports. In a sport-by-sport breakdown, one would learn that baseball (365), basketball (486), bowling (30), cross-country (119), football (94), golf (219), gymnastics (6), ice hockey (18), lacrosse (15), marathon (6), skiing (13), soccer (127), swimming and diving (31), tennis (222), indoor (58) and outdoor (161) track, and wrestling (90) teams competed for NJCAA championships.

You can see that the revenue-producing sport of basketball is clearly the greatest junior college commitment for both women and men; however, this information will make the scholarship seekers in all areas aware that their individual sport specialty is played in the junior college level of competition and that the opportunity exists.

To locate participants I'd suggest that you write for *The Official Handbook and Casebook of the N.J.C.A.A.*, P.O. Box 7305, Colorado Springs, Colorado 80933, or call 303-590-9788. The 1987–1988 revision costs $5.00 for the copy.

The junior college has served as a great proving ground for many outstanding athletes over the years. The foremost player who comes to mind is O.J. Simpson, who went to San Francisco City College, transferred to the University of Southern California, and went on to earn a spot in the NFL Hall of Fame.

By the way, Yogi Berra is a major league baseball Hall of Fame member for his playing ability, not his diction. But I believe in what he said—Your search isn't over until you want it to be. Good luck!

Chapter XIV
Questions Frequently Asked by Athletes and Their Parents

1. Do you recommend a year of preparatory school for my son (or daughter) if he (or she) doesn't earn a scholarship?

Preparatory schools are located in each geographical section of the country. Many offer complete athletic programs; however, most specialize in a specific emphasis sport. It is my opinion that these emphasis sport programs are generally installed to attract more students to the school, not necessarily to be a "proving ground" for athletes.

Many athletes attend preparatory schools each year. The advantage of playing a higher level of competition is obvious, especially for the athlete who comes from a small high school program. The late maturing athlete will probably benefit most. I have always viewed the preparatory school experience as "second chance" experience. The athlete who may have experienced problems in the classroom or on the playing field can utilize a fresh start in the preparatory school environment.

Probably the most negative aspect to be found with attending a preparatory institution is its cost to attend. Since preparatory school programs offer no grant-in-aid money, I suggest that each athlete considering a preparatory school do a cost analysis and weigh the associated pluses and minuses. Remember that all work will earn no transfer of academic credit to a college program. After completing a preparatory school year, each participant will start over as a freshman in the junior college or four year institution in which he enrolls.

If the financial expense is not a negative consideration, then a preparatory school experience can create advantages. The four year colleges like to recruit the prep institutions because prep students do not lose any college athletic eligibility and are more than likely better prepared for college life because they have been away from home for a year. This maturity is important to athletic programs who look for athletes who will fit into the productive playing roles as freshmen.

2. What good are junior colleges? Do they offer an athlete a sound opportunity to display his or her talents?

Accredited junior colleges are a good way to begin your college career if a four year scholarship offer does not present itself. The junior college generally provides an experienced coach or coaching staff to offer good skill-related instruction. Financial aid is usually available. Athletic grants are available, depending on your skills and the specific junior college's needs.

The best factor of junior college play is that the student can begin to work toward a four year degree, since many of the academic credits taken in the junior college will transfer to a degree program at a four year institution. The junior college programs are extremely well recruited by four year colleges looking for mature, capable athletes who can provide immediate help to a program.

The only negative factor of attending a junior college rests with athletic eligibility. The athlete exhausts two years of athletic eligibility if he completes his junior college career. The graduated junior college athlete must be very interested in selecting a four year institution who has great immediate needs for his services, since he or she will have only two remaining years of eligibility upon matriculation to a four year institution.

3. May I sign with two different colleges?

Yes, provided that the two colleges do not honor one another's grant-in-aid. By signing two different grants you may receive adverse publicity. My best advice is to wait until you have finalized your investigations of various colleges. Then sign with the one you feel is best for you.

4. I have already signed a conference grant-in-aid, and the recruiter wants me to sign another form—the National Letter of Intent. What does this mean?

The NCAA asks each athlete to sign a binder to solidify the agreement. This binder is the National Letter of Intent. The letter of Intent only declares your final intentions. It is not a grant-in-aid. Schools honoring the National Letter of Intent will be listed on the back of the contract form.

5. I have signed a conference grant-in-aid and National Letter of Intent with College G. The United States Military Academy recruiter tells me that the Academy doesn't honor either contract. Is this true?

Yes. U.S. military institutions do not honor the Letter of Intent. Many times applicants to the military institutions do not know whether or not they will be accepted for admission until well after the Letter of Intent is issued. If you are considering a military institution you should inform the other college recruiters of your intentions.

The National Letter of Intent is also not honored by some other colleges around the country. The same problem may arise if these colleges are recruiting you. To know who honors the Letter of Intent, read the back side of the form. It will clearly indicate the colleges honoring the binder.

6. I thought that all scholarships were for four years at a time. Is this true? If it isn't true, why?

Although some four year scholarships are still awarded by NAIA affiliates, they are obsolete within the NCAA organization. When the HEW Title IX bill passed, it caused athletic departments across the country to place more emphasis on women's athletics. This placed a greater financial burden on the institutions across the country. Title IX plus the general inflationary economic conditions which prevailed in the 70s made athletic directors take measures to reduce expenses created by the rising cost in athletics. One of the first measures was to reduce the number of years in a scholarship so the schools would only be responsible for one year at a time.

7. The one year renewable scholarship doesn't guarantee us anything but one year at a time. Why couldn't colleges cut into their own pocketbooks instead of ours?

Remember that college athletics is a business. Colleges have trimmed their budgets by (1) offering a limited number of scholarships in each sport, (2) setting maximum sizes for coaching staffs (at one time), (3) setting maximum travel squads and (4) altering recruiting policies in an attempt to pare costs. The one year renewable scholarship is an example of the colleges' awareness of the ever-increasing athletic budgets around the country.

8. No one in my area of the country offers a grant-in-aid for my sport. What recourse do I have?

I suggest that you read "The Helping Hands" chapter in this book for ideas about how to locate colleges and how to market your abilities.

9. One recruiter keeps telling me about the off-campus recreational advantages of his college. How important is this consideration?

The value is completely up to you. I might add, however, that the most important considerations in selecting a college are outlined in great detail in the chapter "Selecting a College."

Athletes today are usually involved in year-round training

programs. This training, coupled with academic demands, leaves little room for the "glamorous" considerations like snow skiing or utilizing the nearby beach.

10. My parents think that my selection reflects a poor decision. They do not want to agree to sign my grant-in-aid contract. What should I do?

I suggest that you sit down to explain your reasons in great detail. Be open and frank about your evaluation. Sometimes some underlying experiences in your campus visitation will give you concrete evidence that one college is a better place for you. Ask your parents to openly discuss their recommendation. Use the observations made during your campus visit to support your reasons and final analysis. I feel if both you and your parents are objective about the decision, there will be little problem in getting together.

11. I am a sophomore in high school. Is it too early to begin my search for the proper college?

Yes. Concentrate your efforts in improving your athletic skills on the playing field and your study habits in the classroom.

12. Do you think summer camps can help an athlete win a scholarship?

Let me answer this with two remarks: (1) summer camps are good because they give an athlete an opportunity to develop the skills of a particular sport. The skills and added experience will help to develop the innate abilities of the athlete. In this respect, the camps are good. (2) No senior athlete is allowed to participate in a summer camp; college recruiting rules prohibit senior participation. But any athlete who can exhibit a high degree of proficiency is certainly going to attract attention to the camp leaders. If the camp is conducted by a high school staff, the staff members will almost certainly be aware of the athlete's talents and recommend his or her name to college recruiters. If the camp is conducted by college coaches, the athlete who displays better than average ability will almost certainly earn a recruiting visit. Each college-level coach who has the opportunity to observe the athlete's skills and talents in a camp situation will already be aware of the athlete's ability when making all-important scholarship decisions.

Although summer instructional sports camps can be a good experience, they are a lot of hard work and can sometimes be rather expensive. The work and expense may be outweighed, however. The athlete may learn a different perspective and some new techniques to aid his or her performance. As for helping to earn a scholarship, any coach who recognized exceptional talent will almost always make a further investigation of the gifted athletes' performances in game-type situations.

13. Is it easier to earn a scholarship at a winning college?

NO. Whether the school presently enjoys success or not, each school seeks athletes who can enhance the fortunes of the program. It is safe to say, however, that athletes who have their pick of colleges will tend to choose the winning programs. It is for this reason alone that good programs continue to be good programs and the demand will make that winning situation more difficult to attain.

14. Does the size of the college usually mean that it gives more scholarships?

Not necessarily. There are many colleges with high student enrollments who choose not to emphasize athletics. Conversely, many colleges with smaller enrollments choose to participate at the highest levels of athletics, creating a larger (scholarship) budget.

15. One college has made offers to me that exceed the value of a grant-in-aid. Who can I turn to for advice?

My strongest recommendation is to alert both your parents and your coach about the wrongdoings. Have them contact (by phone or letter) the national offices affiliated by the college. The affiliation will be either NCAA, NAIA, or NJCAA. An offer over and above room, board, tuition and books may lead to your losing either your scholarship or your eligibility.

16. I have signed a grant-in-aid with College R. Since the signing I have been invited to a postseason all-star game. Should I participate?

Ask the coaches at College R. Most colleges will welcome the opportunity of having one of its new signees participate. The answer will then become an individual agreement between you and your future college.

17. If I agree to one year renewable grant-in-aid, what happens to me if I am injured in my second or third year? Can I lose my scholarship?

The question of the college's policy toward athletic injury should be asked of the recruiter before you ever sign a grant-in-aid. If you have any doubts of the college's integrity, call some of the parents of players already in that particular program to ask how the college has dealt with this problem in the past.

Your coach may also be a reliable source of information. He is in contact with other coaches who may have sent players to that same college. Ask your coach to help you investigate this question as it specifically pertains to each school recruiting your athletic services.

18. Is it safe to assume that all colleges fly via chartered airlines to all away games?

It is not safe to assume anything. Each college you deal with will be slightly different from the next. Investigate the mode of travel just as you might investigate your opportunity to play early. All considerations are important considerations. One point: Each sport at the same university is funded differently. The basketball team may fly via charter but the baseball team may take a bus or van to play the same opponent.

19. How far do most athletes travel from home in selecting a college?

Read the chapter "A Survey of Former Athletes." This survey discovered that the average distance traveled from home to campus was 237 miles. The answer is purely an individual preference since one athlete traveled one mile to college and another elected to travel 2500 miles.

20. What is a "redshirt"?

"Redshirting" is a term assigned to an athlete who has been granted an additional year of athletic eligibility. Although different colleges observe different conference-related or national affiliation–related rules, an athlete has five years to use four years of eligibility. An ineligible freshman's eligibility cannot be waived; however, if a player practices but does not play in any games in a given season, the college does not have to count that year toward his four years of eligibility.

Another reason for redshirting an athlete is because of an injury. If an athlete plays in two football games or less and applies for an injury hardship, he can be granted a redshirt year or be awarded a year's eligibility to replace his injured season—unless he is already in the fifth year. Each different sport will have a slightly different total number of games an athlete can play and still qualify for an injury-related redshirt award.

The ultimate decision is up to the university or college you attend. If you want this protection, ask the recruiter if the college he represents does redshirting.

21. What are the frequently mentioned "core courses"?

The NCAA Division I member institutions will follow a new set of guidelines for all incoming freshmen who matriculate after August 1, 1986. They will utilize 11 core courses to qualify for general acceptance to a university and to qualify for freshman playing eligibility. The course requirements are listed on page 106 of this book.

I strongly suggest that you write the NCAA for the "Guide to New College Freshman Eligibility Requirements for NCAA Division I Institutions." For the most up-to-date information write to the NCAA, P.O. Box 1906, Mission KS 66201 or call 913-384-3220.

22. I want to be a professional athlete. What will College X do to help me reach this goal?

In the movie *Rocky III* Apollo Creed says to the protagonist, "Rocky, you *fight great,* but I'm a *great fighter.*" That says it all. No one knows what you are going to be one, two, three, or four years from today. For nicely prepared information regarding this subject, I would suggest that you write the NCAA for the booklet "A Career in Professional Sports: Guidelines That Make Dollars and Sense." It may be the best 22¢ you've ever spent. It will discuss new eligibility rules which are directly related to a former professional athlete who wants to redirect toward a collegiate lifestyle.

23. What should I wear to visit your campus?

Shine your shoes, comb your hair, dress neatly. Remember, you may be the guest of honor today, but you are creating your first impression as a success of tomorrow.

24. How do I find out recruiting rules as written by the NAIA?

The NAIA sponsors a membership of over 500 institutions who compete for championships in a total of 23 sports for men and women. If you are interested in eligibility regulations, tryout rules, recruitment policies or financial assistance policies, write for "A Guide for the College Bound Student," by the NAIA, 1221 Baltimore Avenue, Kansas City, MO 64105. The telephone number is 816-842-5050.

25. No one in my family has ever gone to college or no one in my family has ever played sports in college. What should I look for in making my decision?

Good, honest question! More people should be as straightforward. My answer is to read this book in its entirety. There is something in every chapter for you to learn and have an opportunity to reflect the principles toward your particular situation.

26. How can I locate a junior college who participates in my sport?

Call the National Junior College Athletic Association in Colorado Springs, Colorado at 303-590-9788 or write to them at P. O. Box 7305, Colorado Springs, CO 80933-7305 and ask to purchase the "Official Handbook and Casebook of the NJCAA." It will answer this question and many more.

27. How does a college staff make its final decision as to which athlete to take into its program?

Each college program utilizes a slightly different philosophy, but I think it would be very helpful to the reader to have a concrete example. Bobby Cremins, the respected men's basketball coach at Georgia Tech, cites the following selection criteria:

- Athletic ability and quickness—does he have the tools to play major college basketball?
- Academic potential—does he have the high school background and is he willing to work toward a degree?
- Character—does the athlete have his priorities in order? Is he honest?
- Unselfishness—is he a team player?
- Attitude—is he willing to work on his weaknesses to improve? Can he play a role?

Appendix A
Résumé Checklist

1. Compile pertinent information about the prospective scholarship candidate. Record the information on a piece of stencil paper so mimeographed copies can be made in abundant numbers, or have it typed neatly and photocopied.

2. Include the athlete's name, address and phone number.

3. Indicate the athlete's height, weight and any measured indicator of his footspeed (clocked time), position played, weight classification or event.

4. Indicate grade point average, class rank, ACT or SAT test results. If the athlete has not taken the SAT or ACT tests, indicate the date the athlete expects to take the test.

5. List any records, "all-state" teams, and special awards received.

6. Be sure to include any individual "off-season" workout accomplishments the athlete has achieved. This may include marks in

weight lifting exercies, vertical jumps, push-ups, bench jumps, shuttle run, President's Council Fitness Testing, etc.

7. Mention athlete's unusual leadership characteristics.

8. Do not hesitate to compare the athlete's favorable attributes to former successful athletes attending the high school.

9. Mention any other pertinent information which demonstrates outstanding capabilities, citizenship, Mr. Hustle, father/mother was a collegiate performer at College X, etc.

10. Include completed team schedule with dates and starting times.

11. Make it clear that films and/or videotapes are available upon request. Include the player's uniform/jersey number.

12. State high school, coach's name, high school telephone number, and comments.

Appendix B
Select-O-Gram

	College A	College B	College C	College D	College E	College F
Academic Atmosphere						
1. Academic image of the college						
2. Does school have your intended major?						
3. Can you enlarge or specialize in great detail on your intended major?						
4. Number of students in average classroom						
5. Curriculum change in sophomore or junior year						
6. Any facility to arrange class schedule to avoid athletic-academic conflict?						
7. Study hall facilities and enforced study time for freshmen						
8. Does athletic department provide tutoring?						
9. Athlete graduation ratio						
10. Athletic department's attitude toward academics						
Social Life						
11. Are you comfortable around the team members?						
12. How are the nonathletes you met?						
13. Are there any social stigmas about athletes?						
14. Any social advantages to athletes?						
15. Campus entertainment						
16. In-town entertainment						

Athletic Facilities

17. Locker room area
18. Training room facilities
19. Convenience to and from practice and class
20. Practice areas
21. Game facilities
22. Coaches' offices and meeting area
23. Facility emphasis in your sport vs. the other sports
24. Athletic housing facilities

Your Health

25. Food—quality and quanity
26. Adequate use of trainers
27. Competent medical staff for consultation
28. Campus hospital or infirmary
29. Community hospital facilities
30. Insurance protection from injuries
31. Quality protective devices or equipment provided by college
32. Your dormitory room

The Athletic Staff
33. The athletic department
34. Sports information director
35. Dormitory supervisor

Your Sport
36. Head coach and staff
37. Team's tradition and won-lost record
38. Position you are being recruited to play
39. Team's style of offense or defense
40. Opportunity to play early
41. Opportunity to play a second sport
42. Media recognition
43. Competitive schedule
44. The other athletes
45. Community interest/fan support

The Campus

46. Number of miles to and from home
47. Pleasant atmosphere for higher education
48. Sufficient library at your access?
49. Can you walk to all points of the campus?
50. Distance from campus housing to classrooms
51. Distance from classrooms to athletic facilities
52. On-campus facility to wash clothes?
53. Do you need an automobile?

Administrative

54. Will you lose your scholarship if you are permanently disabled?
55. Campus—too big or small?
    College—too big or small?
56. Long-range building plans
57. Short-range improvements to facilities
58. Coaches' guidance
59. Guidance counselors
60. Parental guidance

Total Evaluation

Point Total College A	Point Total College B	Point Total College C	Point Total College D	Point Total College E	Point Total College F

Appendix C
A Survey of Former Athletes

College sport(s) played: _____

School attended: _____ Affiliation (NCAA, Jr. Col., NAIA)

Male _____ Female _____

Number of miles from home to your college campus: _____

Please indicate the number of scholarship offers you received from high school by circling the best response.

A. Walk-on   C. 4-6
B. 1-3   D. More than 7

Number of full-scholarship offers? _____

Below is a list of 25 reasons athletes may choose a college or university. Please list in *Column A* the reasons that you chose your college *before* you attended. In *Column B* list the things you would recommend after having finished your career:

a. academic curriculum offered
b. recommendation of high
   school coach
c. recommendation of friend
d. recommendation of alumni
e. went through scouting service
f. recommendation of former
   teammate
g. recommendation of
   girlfriend/boyfriend
h. geographical location
i. head coach of school recruiting
   you
j. athletic tradition of school
k. recruiter of school recruiting
   you
l. school's athletic facilities
m. impression from campus
   visitation

n. graduation ratio of athletes
o. parental influence
p. school's schedule of games
q. style of athletic teams—offense
   or defense
r. team's won/lost record
s. media recognition and
   exposure
t. promise of summer
   employment
u. promise of employment after
   graduation
v. opportunity to play a second
   sport
w. opportunity to play a certain
   position
x. opportunity to play early
y. rapport with coaching staff of
   your school
z. other _____

Appropriate ranking (1-10) in each column

COLUMN A
BEFORE ATTENDING COLLEGE

**Top Ten in Order of
Preference**

1. _____
2. _____
3. _____
4. _____
5. _____
6. _____
7. _____
8. _____
9. _____
10. _____

COLUMN B
*AFTER GRADUATION FROM
COLLEGE*
**Top Ten in Order of
Preference**

1. _____
2. _____
3. _____
4. _____
5. _____
6. _____
7. _____
8. _____
9. _____
10. _____

Index

GLASSBORO STATE COLLEGE

DATE DUE		
S 10-96		
DEC 12 1999		
10/12/01		
OCT 24 2001		
NOV 12 2001		
GAYLORD No. 2333		PRINTED IN U.S.A.